Praise for *Pitch Perfect*

"The book is terrific. It's a very clear, very concrete guide to virtually every aspect of dealing with the news media, right down to blogs and Twitter. But what struck me as most unusual—and potentially most valuable—is its pitch-perfect and lucid presentation of how journalists look at stories and sources and the whole process. It's failure to understand that part of the equation that most often derails potentially effective efforts at communication between the academy and the media. With this book as a guide, that doesn't have to happen. Wonderful job."

—**Richard Cooper**, *former Deputy Bureau Chief and News Editor of the Los Angeles Times Washington Bureau*

"As an academic publisher, I work with hundreds of scholars, encouraging them to communicate their research to the widest audience possible. Each of our authors stands to benefit greatly from Bill Tyson's book, which explains to scholars how they can best share their findings without dumbing down their message. With clear examples and telling anecdotes from across the academic disciplines, Tyson gives faculty a map for transcending their circle of peers and spreading the key points of their research to a larger public."

—**Marlie Wasserman**, *Director, Rutgers University Press*

"This is a remarkable work, a how-to guide to effective media relations by a pro who has seen it all and done it all. It is a brisk, entertaining tour of a largely misunderstood world and a practical and pragmatic primer on how to flourish in it. Now, instead of talking to people about the precepts of media relations, I will simply hand them this book."

—**Don Hale**, *Vice President for Public Affairs, The University of Texas at Austin*

"Do you want media attention? Then read Bill Tyson's *Pitch Perfect*. Better than anything else I've read, Tyson teaches strategies for presenting yourself effectively to both old and new media. He shows you how and he helps you understand why. Even better, he gives sound advice on building constructive, professional relationships with reporters, editors and bloggers that can pay off in the future."

—**Douglas Bennett**, *President, Earlham College*

"Reading this book is like sitting down to a long, pleasurable conversation with your own private media consultant. Chapter by chapter, you learn everything from the deceptively simple task of how to frame clear and compelling media messages to preparing for a media interview. Bill Tyson's eminently readable and useful book is a must-read for those scholars, researchers, and academic leaders who recognize that strategic communications planning is not an option, but rather a critical aspect of their ongoing work."

> —*Joan Dassin*, *Executive Director, Ford Foundation International Fellowships Program*

"In a time of growing scientific, technological and ethical complexity in all aspects of our lives, the need for researchers and the academic community to reach out to the public has never been more important. *Pitch Perfect* provides easy access for the interested, but hesitant academic to get involved in some of the most important national and international conversations of our time. Bill Tyson has provided the tools for getting important information off the sidelines and into the national dialogue without compromising objectivity and scholarship."

> —*Thomas S. Litwin*, *Ph.D. Director, Clark Science Center, Smith College*

PITCH PERFECT

PITCH PERFECT

Communicating with Traditional and Social Media for Scholars, Researchers, and Academic Leaders

WILLIAM TYSON

Foreword by Robert Zemsky

STERLING, VIRGINIA

COPYRIGHT © 2010 BY STYLUS
PUBLISHING, LLC.

Published by Stylus Publishing, LLC
22883 Quicksilver Drive
Sterling, Virginia 20166-2102

**Library of Congress
Cataloging-in-Publication Data**
Tyson, William, 1949-
Pitch perfect : communicating with traditional and
social media for scholars, researchers, and
academic leaders / William Tyson ; foreword by
Robert Zemsky.—1st ed.
    p.   cm.
    Includes bibliographical references and index.
    ISBN 978-1-57922-333-5 (pbk. : alk. paper)
    1. Universities and colleges—Public relations—
United States.   2. Communication in education—
United States.   3. Mass media andeducation—
United States.   4. College teachers—Professional
relationships—United States.   I. Title.
LB2342.8.T97   2010
659.2'937873—dc22
2009052302
13-digit ISBN: 978-1-57922-333-5 (paper)

Printed in the United States of America

All first editions printed on acid free paper
that meets the American National Standards
Institute Z39-48 Standard.

Bulk Purchases

Quantity discounts are available for use in
workshops and for staff development.
Call 1-800-232-0223

First Edition, 2010

10 9 8 7 6 5 4 3 2 1

To Kris, Andy, Alec, Will, and Joe

CONTENTS

ACKNOWLEDGMENTS

Writing this book was a journey that I started alone, but as I soon realized, it was only for a moment. I quickly found it would be a road traveled with family, colleagues, and friends. It was their stories and my experiences with them that I would tell. Many of these people were present to help me in the writing of this book through their support, insight, feedback, and friendship.

Thank you, Kris, for your love, unwavering support, and beautiful smile after reading my first draft that told me I was on the way. Thanks to my sons, Andy, Alec, Will, and Joe, who never seemed to doubt that Dad should write a book. Their response to the publisher's call: "Cool."

To Ellen Wert, whose discussion with publisher John von Knorring about the need for a practical guide on communications for scholars and her recommendation that he contact me to write it was the act of kindness and thoughtfulness that inspired this work.

To Ben Daviss, Don Hale, Dick Cooper, and Jeff Hanna for their editing support of early drafts of the book and for their helpful comments that added depth to the discussion. To Bob Zemsky, George Kuh, Marlie Wasserman, Doug Bennett, Joan Dassin, and Tom Litwin, who also generously gave of their time to read early drafts and provided rich feedback and support.

To Kay McClenney, Brooks Hansen, Sharon Begley, Russ Edgerton, and Peter Ewell who joined me on this journey, listening to my thoughts and discussing ideas with me about the content and direction for the book.

To Joe Tyson, photographer and youngest son, who has great camera skills and an artist's eye.

To John von Knorring, for his gentle direction and adroit publishing talents that focus on sharing knowledge and advancing academic and professional excellence.

To Maggy Ralbovsky, a valued colleague at Morrison & Tyson Communications. To Pat Kingsbury, along with Maggy, who helped me find time to write my *Moby Dick*. To the memory of Dave Morrison, a wonderful partner with whom I shared this journey so many years ago. To Fred Gehrung, who recognized early the rich stories that higher education has to tell.

To my parents.

I give my deep appreciation to all.

FOREWORD

She was as exasperated as I was angry. In those days, Ann Duffield headed University Relations for the University of Pennsylvania. Among the many cats she was expected to herd was an in-house weekly aimed at the university's professional and clerical staff. At Ann's suggestion, the paper's editor had approached me requesting an interview on coming trends in higher education. I agreed to the interview, the editor dutifully appeared, and wrote an article that did nothing to polish my image for either probity or prescience. I knew Ann well enough to remonstrate with her on the hatchet job I thought the story had done on me. The next day, Ann appeared in my office, recorder in hand, and played me the tape of my interview. What I heard was appalling—a wandering monologue that made little sense, frequently contradicted itself, and left the clear impression that I just liked to talk—about everything and everybody. Ann clicked off the recorder and said simply, "Boy, do you need help."

The next year Ann was helping us establish the Pew Higher Education Roundtable, a collection of some 20-plus Pooh-Bahs whose quarterly gatherings were scheduled to provide the substance for a series of essays to be published as the first issues of *Policy Perspectives*. Ann was the principal designer of the publication as well as the person we had enlisted to help us encourage the media to be interested in what the Roundtable was saying. She asked all the right questions. Are you really ready to talk to the media? Do you know what you want to say, and do you have the self-discipline to stay on message? And, having reminded me of my disastrous interview of the preceding year, Ann ended by asking, "Are you really ready to ask for help?"

And that is how I came to know and depend on Bill Tyson. In the mid-1980s, Ann had engaged Bill to provide counsel for Penn's media coverage. Bill had just started his company with David Morrison—Morrison & Tyson Communications—and was just building his reputation as someone who understood how the media functioned, what it took to get noticed, and how not to simply assume others would be interested in what you have to say. As his business grew, Bill had the luxury to become kind of picky as to whom his clients were—he not only wanted them to behave, he wanted them to have something important to say. Part of what Bill helped Ann and me to do for the Pew Higher Education Roundtable was to get the right people to notice what we were doing. One of his first coups was to get us involved with the *Washington Post*, which we hoped would be interested in the inaugural issue of *Policy Perspectives*. In fact, the *Post* made our essay on college costs the subject of an editorial on the very day we were appearing before the assembled presidents of the Association of American Universities, where we argued for a greater focus on cost containment. (One of the lessons I took from that extraordinary piece of serendipity was that Bill also had an "in" with the lords of the dice, though he strenuously denies any connection whatsoever).

Bill's promises to those of us he has worked with are always the same. "I can't speak for you. I can't promise that what you have to say will be of interest to the media. I have no say on how a story is placed. And, by the way, if you can write an op-ed that focuses on your important idea, you will make my task that much easier."

Though he never promises, he can open doors if you are prepared to walk through them knowing what you are about, knowing what you have to say, and knowing why your message is important.

I have now benefited from Bill Tyson's counsel—and that is what he offers—for more than twenty years. Along the way, he has taught me a host of invaluable lessons that, in turn, have become the substance of the volume you are about to read. In important ways, *Pitch Perfect* is a much-needed primer telling faculty readers what they need to know if they want to make what they know and have discovered important to other people. But this volume is also much more, in that it offers Bill's reflections and musings on what it is like working with faculty who, when confronted by the members of the media, often appear to be deer caught in someone else's headlights. We storm, we fuss, we think the failure of others to notice how important our ideas and findings are is a product of their shortsightedness rather than a reflection of our hubris. Read this volume closely and you will understand what works and what doesn't and why. Just as he does in his practice, Bill the author can help you scale your expectations and focus your energies. Here is a volume truly chock full of practical advice offered in a context that helps make the mysterious rational.

There is a final aspect to Bill Tyson's work—he is an exquisite listener and practiced learner. Bill is forever telling those of us he works with just how much he learns from each of us. No doubt some of those with whom Bill works take his compliments as a good example of what one does in order to build and maintain a successful media consulting practice. I know better. Over these twenty-plus years, I have watched Bill develop an ever-deeper understanding of what the academy is about and what makes us academics tick. If he will allow me, I think I have contributed to that process, in part by reminding Bill that what a research scholar wants is to have his work noticed in order that it can have the impact it deserves.

Long ago, I told Bill the story of my being interviewed by Arnie Eisen, now the Chancellor of the Jewish Theological Seminary in New York, but then a senior editor and columnist for the *Daily Pennsylvanian*, the University of Pennsylvania's student daily. Eisen had come to interview me when I was a young assistant professor. He wanted me to talk about the perils and pressures of a world in which you perished if you didn't publish. What I remembered telling him then, and repeated to Bill years later, was that I wasn't so much afraid of the pressure to publish as I was worried that I wouldn't be able to. I had spent a half-dozen years becoming an expert on American colonial history, and I decidedly had things to say, things to communicate. That was the underlying moral of the story. Being a faculty member and researcher is as much about communication as it is discovery. There is a power as well as an arrogance attached to new ideas well presented. My advice to Bill was not to let faculty claim that we didn't want the limelight. What we all want is to make sure that our ideas reach the right audience as quickly as possible.

The book you are about to read is testament to just how good Bill Tyson is at providing the right kind of advice as well as making the right kind of contacts to spread one's ideas. Enjoy.

Dr. Robert Zemsky
Education Professor and
Chairman of The Learning Alliance for Higher Education
University of Pennsylvania

CHAPTER ONE

Telling Your Story

IS IT A GOOD REPORT IF IT'S NOT READ?

Thousands of scholarly papers and books are written each year. Many have value to audiences beyond the academy and the institutions supporting these efforts. Yet most new works and their ability to influence change go unheard. "Ideas no longer score points," says one university professor. "Their impact must be amplified to be noticed in an increasingly complicated world."

This book is written for scholars, researchers, and academic leaders who have a passion to share their knowledge outside the classroom, laboratory, or institution. They want to make a difference and believe the value of the information they possess and ideas they offer have a public importance. *Pitch Perfect* is a practical guide to communicating knowledge and ideas to broader audiences.

Dust settles quickly on many scholarly compositions, the knowledge they offer buried within their pages. Communicating new ideas and findings are often afterthoughts for many scholars and researchers. They assume or hope their published works will rise to the top of conversation among their peers and the public. They rest in the belief that their reports, scholarly papers, or books, often deep in jargon, will find their way to key audiences, will be read with anticipation, and enter into professional and public discourse. Often the reality is disappointment in the lack of awareness and impact their work achieves. "Knowing what you know doesn't get you anywhere. Telling people what you know does," said Kay McClenney, director of the Center for Community College Student Engagement at The University of Texas at Austin. McClenney's strong media outreach has generated important national discussions about higher education quality and access.

Scholars and researchers increasingly are being asked by funders to develop communication plans for programs receiving support. These organizations and institutions recognize that the value of a scholar's work lies not only in the new findings but also in communicating the implications of this knowledge to key audiences and the public. Without good communication, many important works do not achieve the desired effects of advancing knowledge and creating new dialogue.

Whether your goal is to reach specific target audiences or the broader public, early and thoughtful communication planning is essential to having your story heard. And the key to a strong communication plan is knowing how to present your work to the media. Good media coverage connects you to important audiences and the public. It broadens awareness and understanding of your messages. It amplifies your voice and further validates your good work.

My work in the field of communications and media relations spans more than 30 years. It began in Hawaii where I developed advertising campaigns for a major newspaper. Returning to the mainland, I entered the health care field as a consultant, writing

marketing and press material to support hospital building programs, and codirecting campaigns. Having had success in these
efforts, I was asked to direct a capital campaign that helped lead
to the opening of a regional university in New England. I was
witnessing in my career that the value of defining a strong story
and communicating it to key audiences was essential to creating
meaningful change. I also saw the media's huge influence in this
process. Choosing between development and communications, I
opted for the latter and entered the field of national media relations as a consultant and then became owner of a leading firm
serving colleges, universities, policy institutes, and foundations.
Over many years, I have worked with hundreds of professors,
researchers, directors, and presidents, helping them shape and tell
their stories, which have informed the public, advanced dialogue,
and created important and meaningful change.

Coming to Terms

Some scholars believe it is inappropriate for them to take an active
role in advancing their work outside academic circles, particularly
to and through the mainstream media. "I don't care about marketing and PR," they say with pride. They see such actions as *spin*, a
presentation of their work in a biased or distorted fashion. This
view puts negative connotations on terms that in their true sense
are quite different. Simply put, true marketing and PR means
thoughtful, honest communications that reach key audiences. It is
giving greater voice to your messages, creating awareness and
deeper understanding of issues, building trust, and promoting
action.

Others feel modest and are hesitant to be seen as self-promoters.
As a friend occasionally reminds me, "Get over yourself." If your

work has a broader public importance or you can help interpret local, national, or world events, or offer expert opinion on matters of professional and public importance or interest, share your thoughts. Instill knowledge. It does not need to be about you but rather the importance of your insight and information.

This is not a new concept. You are "the world's eye" and "the world's heart," said Ralph Waldo Emerson in his 1837 address, "The American Scholar," which he delivered in Cambridge, Massachusetts, to the Phi Beta Kappa Society.(1) "Emerson envisioned the American scholar as a person who would do whatever possible to communicate ideas to the world, not just fellow intellectuals," wrote Jeffrey R. Di Leo, editor and publisher of the *American Book Review*.(2)

Thomas Litwin, director of the Smith College Clark Science Center, believes that "faculty members should feel obliged to share what we know with the public." Litwin retraced the 9,000-mile route of the 1899 E. H. Harriman Expedition scientific voyage along the Alaska coast. This work became the basis of a Public Broadcasting System (PBS) documentary, book, magazine articles, blogs, and classroom instructional guide, giving viewers and readers a deeper understanding of the ecological and societal changes that have occurred in Alaska over the last century. "We as scholars hold important information that can benefit the common good; we should feel obligated to reach the largest audience we can to advance important issues," Litwin said. An added incentive for many scholars is that by having their work noted, whether in professional journals or in the mainstream media, they are helping to advance the name, recognition, and reputation of their institutions. The public's positive perception of a college, university, or policy institute often is based on the good work and insight of its researchers, faculty, and scholars whom they observe in the media.

Lee Smith, former *Fortune* senior writer and chief for the magazine's Washington and Tokyo bureaus, wrote in a commentary for the *Chronicle of Higher Education*:

> Faculty members are the experts that the news media often cite. The comments and observations of professors in newspapers like the [*New York*] *Times*, based on their research and expertise, promote the intellectual resources of their institutions and expand every reader's knowledge and understanding of the issue at hand. In addition to what colleges and universities owe their students, faculty members protect and promote a body of knowledge for the benefit of society. That body of knowledge includes the current as well as the traditional: The war in Iraq along with the Peloponnesian, the rise of the middle class in China as well as the decline of the Middle Ages in the West, the retreat of the glaciers in Greenland as well as the fundamentals of physics.(3)

Findings from a 2009 survey I conducted of 95 faculty, scholars, and researchers from 21 colleges, universities, and organizations across the country in which I asked them to rate their overall experiences in dealing with the media were overwhelmingly positive.

- ◆ Local media: 95% of the respondents who had interaction with the local media found it to be a positive to very positive experience.

- ◆ Regional media: 96% of the respondents who had interaction with the regional media found it to be a positive to very positive experience.

- ◆ National media: 95% of the respondents who had interaction with the national media found it to be a positive to very positive experience.

Asked why they choose to interact with the media, they gave the following three leading reasons:

- ◆ to improve public understanding of their areas of expertise

- ◆ to enhance the reputation of their institutions

- ◆ to enjoy talking with people who have an interest in their work

Time, Risk, and Rewards

Earning positive media coverage takes time, and often a lot of it. There are no guarantees of success, and when there are results they can be less than what you were hoping for. It is not uncommon to spend an hour or more on the phone answering a reporter's questions about an issue he or she is covering only to find that you were barely mentioned in the article or not quoted at all. You can generally assume that the reporter did not intend it to be this way. Your contribution to the story may have been well noted in the article before the reporter turned it over to his or her editor who then cut its length so it would fit in the shrinking news space of the publication. Many major newspapers and magazines have made dramatic cuts to their news staffs over the years as well as trimmed the size of their publications, making them narrower, thinner, or both to reduce costs. These actions have resulted in less talent and space to report the news.(4)

Also, good reporting comes from extensive research and choosing the best pieces from a reservoir of data to craft a story. The sum of the information collected informs and directs the reporter, but all the facts, figures, and quotes must then be winnowed for fit and relevance. A good quote is sacrificed for another that the reporter believes can better help tell the story. A quote can be important not only for what is said but also for who is saying it. The person's degree of closeness to the issue, his or her title, employer, gender, and geographic location are some of the added factors the reporter may have considered when choosing one source over another.

According to the editor of one leading newspaper, except for true break-through research, academics are usually just one ingredient to reporting a story. Reporters usually talk to them to get specific expertise, background, or quotes.

Reporters for the most part are not certain what direction their stories will take until all the reporting is in. Editing decisions are then made, and some quotes, sometimes unfortunately yours, are sacrificed over others.

The faculty you often see quoted know this and are willing to take this chance. They find that over time the success of media coverage outweighs the disappointments. And for some, it is more a matter of educating a reporter about an important issue than it is to be quoted. Their goal is to advance the knowledge of the public through their conversations with the media.

One university professor said he didn't mind if his name was mentioned in the press or not. As we planned a series of meetings with reporters, editors, and producers, he said it was more important to him that the media begin to write about issues of cost, quality, and access in higher education—issues he felt needed critical public attention. He supported his message with new research and data, and members of the media and the public responded in making these issues their concerns as well.

Media coverage also comes with risk, most notably in being misquoted or seeing your words presented out of context. It is inherent in the process of two people talking with each other: one person misunderstands what the other said or meant. Yet, in my faculty survey noted earlier, 96% of the respondents rated the accuracy of the media as positive to very positive.

All this being said, the rewards of generating meaningful media coverage can be well worth the time and risk involved, especially when the results of your time spent talking with a reporter leads to major news coverage and advances public dialogue about important issues central to your work. "You're not speaking into an abyss," said Bill Wolff, a national television executive producer, referring to the impact a person can have when appearing on network or cable television. "If just one of the people watching happens to have a blog, it's not just your audience of 100,000 people anymore, it's 100 million people."(5) The Associated Press (AP) tells us, "On any given day, more than half the world's population sees news from AP."(6) Media's reach and its potential to tell your message is phenomenal.

Administrators of the Bill and Melinda Gates Foundation consider media coverage essential in their efforts to improve global health, spending millions to finance health journalism. *PBS NewsHour* received a grant from the Gates foundation for $3.5 million to help its correspondents produce 40 to 50 reports on global health issues. The foundation has donated millions of dollars to support other news outlets as well in reporting health-related news.(7)

Over the years, my media relations work with scholars and researchers has led to public awareness and positive, transforming action on such important and diverse matters as U.S. science education, postundergraduate education in developing countries, world hunger awareness, early childhood education, medical training of family practitioners for America's underserved populations, decreasing infant death, improved teaching and learning in higher education, keeping the night sky dark for astronomers, the Human Genome Project, funding of a national earthquake center, entrepreneurship, economic and cultural student diversity, and communicating/advancing scholarly viewpoints and insights to national and international audiences regarding important matters of science, technology, culture, national and world affairs, business, medicine, health, education, and more.

Astronomer Carl Sagan conveyed "the wonders of the universe to millions of people" through newspaper, magazines, books, and television, developing in many a love for astronomy.(8) *Cosmos*, his 1980s PBS 13-part series that explored the mysteries of the universe, gave meaning to viewers young and old about such astronomical phenomena as Kepler's laws of planetary motion, and involved the public in the debate about whether life exists on Mars. He had the democratic belief that all people have the capacity and interest to learn. He respected their intelligence and gave them a show.

"Carl was a candle in the dark. He was, quite simply, the best educator in the world this century," said Yervant Terzian, chairman of Cornell University's astronomy department. "He touched hundreds of millions of people and inspired young generations to pursue the sciences."(9)

In an interview about popularizing science, Sagan said, "There are at least two reasons why scientists have an obligation to explain what science is all about. One is naked self-interest. Much of the funding for science comes from the public, and the public has a right to know how their money is being spent. If we scientists increase the public excitement about science, there is a good chance of having more public supporters. The other is that it's tremendously exciting to communicate your own excitement to others."(10)

News of the death of noted scientist Robert Jastrow was reported in the *New York Times* with the headline, "Robert Jastrow, Who Made Space Understandable, Dies at 82." In the article, a former student of Jastrow's said, "He had a deep sense of the need to interpret science and make it available to the public." The *Times* reporter noted that Jastrow's "descriptions were sharp and his language clear" as he helped the country to understand the space program, astronomy, earth sciences, and other matters as they related to the country's race to space in the 1960s.(11)

You are the "world's eye" and the "world's heart."(12) Let's get started as we address the best principles in working with the media and being heard.

CASE STUDY: EARLY MEDIA OUTREACH

Launched in 2000, the goal of the National Survey of Student Engagement (NSSE) was to develop measures of effective teaching and learning in America's colleges and universities and to provide the public, particularly high school students, with meaningful information they could use to select a college best for them. The findings of this annual survey were meant to serve as a counterweight to popular magazine college guides that heavily relied on institutional reputation and wealth in determining school rankings.

Staff at NSSE realized from the start that building a strategic communications program to support the initiative would be critical to its success. I was brought in early to work with the NSSE board and director George Kuh, Chancellor's Professor of Higher Education at Indiana University Bloomington. Planning began immediately, focusing on NSSE's key messages and its audiences and how best to reach them. NSSE needed to communicate its importance as an effective diagnostic tool for evaluating teaching and learning in the classroom and its value to institutions and the public.

Communication with the colleges and universities was direct, personal, informative, and frequent. NSSE staff members were tireless in providing as much information they thought would be helpful to institutional researchers, presidents, and key audiences concerning the value and administration of its survey. NSSE's goal was to bring the public into this conversation about measuring college quality based on demonstrated teaching and learning data.

To reach the public and to reinforce its messages and work within the academy, NSSE took its story to the media. The key was to approach the media early, meeting with national reporters, editors, and producers to introduce its story, the upcoming release of its survey findings, and to provide the background and context for why this information was important to higher education and to the public.

The process of meeting individually with the media began months before the public release of the data. As director, Kuh was best able to tell the NSSE story (findings were not yet available, but the rationale and context for the survey could be discussed) and to serve as an ongoing contact for the media as they began to understand and appreciate its significance. Designed to be an important institutional research instrument first, conversations needed to convey this value without becoming too much "inside baseball" for audiences, which were the academic and mainstream media, to appreciate. NSSE also worked to link the discussion about its survey to broader issues of interest to the academy and the public, such as effective teaching and learning practices, evaluating institutional quality, college rankings, and college choice.

The media responded with coverage about NSSE findings and the term *student engagement* and its importance. Stories appeared in the *Chronicle of Higher Education*, *USA Today*, *Christian Science Monitor*, *Time*, on the NBC *Today* show, and other news outlets. This advance media work by NSSE gave reporters an opportunity to understand the story and its significance, and the time to write about it to coincide with the release of the survey findings. Media coverage reinforced and further validated NSSE's significance to its primary audiences on campuses across the country and made the case to the public that there was now a better means to select colleges than focusing on popular magazine rankings. NSSE continues its media outreach with its director and staff serving as expert sources to reporters for their ongoing stories about survey-related topics and by writing journal and opinion pieces that continue to define NSSE's purpose and value. *USA Today* has launched an annual NSSE special in its newspaper and on its Web site that profiles institutional excellence in teaching and learning based on NSSE data and directs readers to NSSE participating schools for added discussion.

NSSE is a model for early media outreach. Often, a project that involves the release of major news requires journalists to have a greater depth of knowledge to fully understand and appreciate its significance. Contacting the media early to alert them to the pending story, along with offering background and context, can make the difference between its being reported or not. The major media have an abundance of news to cover, and all else being relatively equal, the stories they choose are generally the ones that are easiest to report. Don't make it harder for them to select your story because it showed up on someone's desk or computer screen the day of its release and it required a level of understanding the reporter had too little time to develop.

Notes

1. Emerson, R. W. (August 31, 1837). *The American Scholar.* Retrieved February 20, 2008, from Emerson Central: http://www.emersoncentral.com/amscholar.htm

2. Di Leo, J. (2008, February 4). Public Intellectuals, Inc. Retrieved February 18, 2008, from *Inside Higher Ed*: http://www.insidehighered.com/views/2008/02/04/dileo

3. Smith, L. (2008, May 9). The Wealthiest Colleges Should Acquire the New York Times. *Chronicle of Higher Education, 54*(35), p. A32.

4. Project for Excellence in Journalism. (2008). *The State of the News Media 2008: An Annual Report on American Journalism. Overview.* Retrieved April 17, 2008, from http://www.stateofthemedia.org/2008/print able_overview_intro.htm

5. Parker, A. (2008, October 26). At Pundit School, Learning to Smile and Interrupt. Retrieved November 25, 2009, from the *New York Times*: http://www.nytimes.com/2008/10/26/fashion/26pundit.html?_r = 1

6. Associated Press. (2009). *Facts and Figures.* Retrieved October 26, 2008, from http://www.ap.org/pages/about/about.html

7. McNeil Jr., D. (2008, December 9). Global Update. *New York Times*, p. D6.

8. Dicke, W. (1996, December 21). Carl Sagan, an Astronomer Who Excelled at Popularizing Science, Is Dead at 62. Retrieved December 30, 2009, from the *New York Times*: http://www.nytimes.com/learning/general/ onthisday/bday/1109.html?scp = 1&sq = william%20dicke%20carl%20sa gan&st = cse

9. Brand, D. (1996, December 20). *Carl Sagan, Cornell Astronomer, Dies Today (Dec. 20) in Seattle* [Press release]. Retrieved November 9, 2008, from http://www.news.cornell.edu/releases/Dec96/saganobit.ltb.html

10. Dicke, *Carl Sagan.*

11. Schwartz, J. (2008, February 12). Robert Jastrow, Who Made Space Understandable, Dies at 82. Retrieved December 30, 2009, from the *New York Times*: http://www.nytimes.com/2008/02/12/science/space/12jastrow .html?scp = 1&sq = john%20schwartz%20robert%20jastrow&st = cse

12. Emerson, *The American Scholar.*

CHAPTER TWO

How the Media Work

I divide the media into three broad groups: print, broadcast, and
Web 2.0. Print media include professional journals dedicated to
one's discipline or field of expertise, such as *Science*, *Nature*,
American History Review, *Journal of the American Academy of
Religion*, and *Foreign Affairs*. Trade media, print and online, such
as the *Chronicle of Higher Education*, *Inside Higher Education*,
and *Change*, are written for an academic audience and other interested readers. Weekly mainstream news magazines include *Time*
and *Newsweek* and monthly publications such as the *Atlantic* and
Harper's. The major daily national newspapers include the *New
York Times*, *Wall Street Journal*, and *USA Today*. Some regional
papers are the *Boston Globe*, *Chicago Tribune*, and *Dallas Morning News*, and local newspapers' readership market is mostly limited to the town or city they serve.

Broadcast includes television, major networks, and cable and
radio.

Web 2.0, which ushered in social media, increasingly defines the
Web as we know it today, what it is, and what it may become. It

is fast, fluid, and personal, and the number of people it can reach is breathtaking. Blogs, podcasts, and social networking sites such as YouTube and Twitter are the new marketplace for the dissemination of news and ideas.

What drives all media is the story, reporting information that is new and has relevance to their audiences. Dominant areas of news coverage include local, national, and world news; business; politics; science and technology; medicine and health; education; popular culture; and the arts. Editors, producers, writers, reporters, and bloggers make their decision on the stories that make it into print, on the air, or on the Web by asking: Is it new and interesting and will our readers or listeners care? Judging the value of a story, for the most part, is grounded in a professional body of journalism standards. If you want the media to be interested in your work, you need to understand their needs and audiences and whether your story is news.

Earning Media Coverage

Generating media coverage is a science and an art. It is not only having a good story and a plan to tell it but also developing a sense of timing, possessing the skill to tell your story, and having an element of luck. (As Louis Pasteur observed, "Chance favors the prepared mind.")

Successful media relations is a process, not an event. It starts far in advance of writing a press release or contacting a reporter. It is about your following the news and knowing how your expertise or new study adds meaning to the public discourse. Meaningful media coverage is earned, not bought (that's called advertising).

Faculty and other scholars usually contact the media for two reasons: to serve as expert story sources for news and feature articles and to report new research findings of major significance.

Those in the media rely on expert sources to add meaning to their stories. Expert sources are frequently quoted in major news and feature articles and heard on broadcasts. These sources can provide the reader and listener with added knowledge, offering context and insight about the topic being reported. The demand for well-qualified and articulate sources seems to be insatiable as news reporting has moved from the morning newspaper and the evening network newscast to 24/7 cable news and Internet coverage of the events of the day.

Washington Post columnist Jeffrey Birnbaum in an *American Journalism Review* article said that expert sources, as found on America's campuses, "add to the credibility of what [reporters] write."(1)

If your goal is to inform the public and earn media coverage for your scholarly work and expertise, you first need to define your core messages and determine their news value. Ask yourself what people should know about your news and why they should care. Who are your audiences? And what media outlets might best reach them?

If you are introducing new research, you will know its importance and should be able to connect its relevance within your profession and possibly to broader audiences as well. Your colleagues can help as a sounding board. Also, at many institutions you can receive professional advice from the office of communications or a similar department.

However, media coverage is not a right. It is not something everyone deserves or should command. Because you want it does not make it so. Egos need to be checked. Not all new research, programs, and opinion are news and deserve the media's attention.

When a person is quoted or new research makes the news, a sense of "It's all PR" is not uncommon among faculty and campus administrators. It's not. Public relations, or more specifically media relations, can help in identifying a story and communicating it to the press; however, it does not create the news. The key to achieving media coverage is to have a good story to start with.

Sources who always seem to be quoted in the media are there because of their expertise, relevance to the issue being reported, willingness to talk to reporters, accessibility, and their ability to clearly communicate key messages to diverse audiences. They quickly return media calls, know the issues, are good communicators, and are direct and honest in their discussion.

Sure some sources whose expertise is thin slip by and get quoted in the press. However, those in the media realize that often there is no one expert on an issue and some days a story deadline demands going with the source in hand. Though the person interviewed may not be a leading scholar in the field, he or she provided a degree of informed opinion or knowledge for the reporter and was available when needed. As in many situations in life, timing is everything, especially in the news business. Every expert source I know whom media regularly contact makes responding to their calls a high priority. These sources don't let media queries linger until the next day or later in the week to respond. They know the reporter is often on deadline, and even waiting an hour or two can be too late.

Reporting the news has always been about getting the story out fast. No longer waiting to write the story for tomorrow's paper, reporters' deadlines are immediate as they race to post their articles on the Web as the news is breaking. "Eighty percent of success is showing up," said comedian, actor, and director Woody Allen. For effective media relations it might be said that 80% of success is returning the reporter's call promptly.

When I am traveling with faculty, institute directors, or college and university presidents they often use the time between meetings, whether in a taxi or walking down the street, to respond to a reporter's call or e-mail on their BlackBerry or a similar smart-phone device.

One professor didn't even let a transcontinental flight deter him from quickly responding to a journalist's urgent query. The professor "was on a non-stop flight from New York to Los Angeles when he got word I was trying to reach him," wrote the columnist for his article in *USA Today*. "Using an onboard Wi-Fi connection, [the professor] sent me a copy of an article he co-authored on the subject two years ago, along with a cellphone number I could reach him on when he landed."(2)

Getting on the Media's Contact Lists

Reporters, editors, and producers choose their story sources in many of the same ways we might find the name of a good physician or attorney. They ask for recommendations from friends, colleagues at work, and professionals in the field. They conduct Google and other Web searches they hope will lead them to their goal.

Media often look to authors of books, journal articles, opinion articles, and even letters to the editor for sources to contact. In a fast media world, these forums are shortcuts to determining who has something to say and who has the expertise to potentially provide useful background and insight for stories.

"Don't tell me, show me," is what a public radio producer for a national talk show pretty much told me once in my early days of media relations. I had called her to pitch my expert faculty source, an economist, as a guest to discuss the Organization of the Petroleum Exporting Countries. Knowing that I needed to win her attention in the first moments of the conversation, I gave her my elevator pitch (the story in two minutes or less) on why I thought the person I was presenting would be a perfect guest interview for her show. I told her about his PhD and the elite universities he attended. I mentioned the course he teaches that relates to the topic. Capping it off, I gave her my assurance that he would be an excellent interview.

Not moved by my list of dry facts and opinion about his interview skills, the producer cut to the heart of the matter and asked, "Why should I believe you?" Stunned but ready to learn, I asked how they selected their guests. She said that they often look for authors of books, journal articles, and opinion pieces appearing in major publications. They also scan major newspapers and news weeklies, noting who is being quoted on topics of interest to them. Short on staff, they did not always have the time to conduct extensive research to identify leading experts in a particular field and to validate their work. Instead they often looked to other media to do this for them. The author of a *New York Times* opinion article writing about a topic of interest to the show, for example, was a good place to start in the process of identifying a potential guest.

Another early lesson on what the media looks for in selecting a story source came when I was meeting with the science reporter for a major news weekly. As I entered her office she was opening her mail. In her hands was a large, nicely bound expert source guide from a premier research university. She looked at the cover, checked the index, and then tossed the book in her wastebasket. Surprised, I asked why she wouldn't use it, especially since it could be assumed that the university had some of the top experts in the country on its research and teaching staff.

She showed me her Rolodex bulging with story contacts and said she identifies potential sources for her stories by reading science journals, newspapers, and magazines, and through recommendations from experts in the field. What was not of interest to her were expert guides that often were sent from colleges, universities, policy institutes, and others that merely listed a faculty member's name, title, degrees, and area of expertise, such as genetic engineering.

She said that she did not care where a person went to school. More important to her was what an expert has to say and the relevance of his or her work. A home run to her was finding a source who had written a book or journal article on a topic of interest, or demonstrated his or her expertise in other meaningful ways. This might include testifying in a congressional hearing about a piece of legislation related to her story on federal research funding, or being selected as a keynote speaker for a national science conference to talk about new developments in a particular field. Her point was that in a world full of experts, the people who earned her attention as potential story sources were conducting leading research and often connecting their work to professional and public discourse through presentations at professional society meetings, and writing books, journal articles, opinion pieces, and blogs.

And just because you may not be from Harvard or another marquee institution or organization, members of the media say it doesn't matter. They are looking for sources that have something to say and the expertise to back it up. Discussing the characteristics of a news source, a major newspaper senior correspondent said it's not where you are from, it's your expertise that is most important. He added that a good story source responds quickly to a reporter's call, has something to say, and discusses the topic presented. Academics, scholars, and researchers need to address the subject the reporter is asking about, not something else. A reporter is often talking about an idea that the person being interviewed has not thought about. Ideas grow out of news. Finally, he

said that if a source is responsive, a reporter tends to call him or
her back.

Notes

1. Cohen, M. (2005, April/May). The Quote Machines. Retrieved
November 21, 2008, from the *American Journalism Review*: http://www.ajr
.org/article_printable.asp?id = 3857

2. Wickham, D. (2009, February 24). Black as Monkeys? It's Time for
an Adult Conversation. Retrieved December 30, 2009, from *USA Today*:
http://blogs.usatoday.com/oped/2009/02/blacks-as-monke.html

CHAPTER THREE

Getting Started

You want to keep on top of the news. It is not enough to occasionally pick up a newspaper or magazine or scan a news Web site to see what's new. To be effective in working with the media, you need to establish a daily routine of reading key publications. Arguably, the major media's bible is the *New York Times*. The news that appears in the *Times* often sets the agenda for the other media, particularly for broadcast outlets and the Web. Certainly other publications and news services, such as the *Wall Street Journal*, *Washington Post*, *Los Angeles Times,* and AP, also strongly influence public and media agendas, but in my experience the *Times* dominates.

Trade and professional journals targeted to specific fields of study also drive media discussion. Journals such as *Science*, *American Journal of Medicine*, *Nature,* and a host of others are where the mainstream and new media often find their stories.

Tune in to key radio and television news programs such as National Public Radio's (NPR) *All Things Considered* or NBC's *Meet the Press*. Stories presented there can have a life beyond their initial broadcast and be reported by other media. A bureau chief for an international newspaper, for example, told me his editors pick up story ideas from listening to NPR.

Logging on to news aggregators on the Web such as Google and Newser, whose teams of editors and writers cull what they consider to be the most important stories from hundreds of U.S. and international sources and briefly summarize them, will also keep you on top of the news 24/7.

Your reading soon will allow you to build background files on current news developments as they relate to your expertise as well as give you firsthand knowledge of the stories of interest to the media and the reporters covering them.

Contacting the Media

There are no complicated formulas in dealing with the media, just common sense. Like many people, those in the media respect professionalism and hate to have their time wasted. Their job is to report the news, and if you have a good story to tell and you tell it well, then you stand a chance of success.

Before approaching the media with a story, you should have

1. Knowledge about the media outlet and the reporter you are about to contact.
2. A concise understanding of your story.
3. A concise explanation of why your story would be of interest to readers, listeners, or viewers.

The question I receive most often from people wanting to approach the media is should they phone, fax, e-mail, or use snail mail? The answer is yes.

One of the leading magazine science writers in the country tells me that she does not mind receiving a well-targeted (i.e., the caller is familiar with her reporting and her publication) and brief phone call from a scholar or researcher suggesting a story idea. She says, though, that it is even better for the person to send a brief e-mail introducing the story. It is usually more concise than a telephone conversation, and she said if she is interested she'll write back to ask for more information.

A former editorial director for a national business magazine said she welcomed calls to discuss story ideas, yet she was surprised at how few she received. Stories were being sent to her by e-mail and by fax, yet she often preferred to discuss ideas over the phone. "Please tell people to pick up the phone and call me," she said. "It is amazing to me how many people don't do this anymore with their story ideas, and because I am on the road so often, I can't get through all of the e-mail."

You never know how best to reach a reporter until you ask. If you are contacting a reporter with an idea you believe is truly of story interest, he or she should not mind a well-prepared telephone call or e-mail to open the discussion.

The best media relations come from developing a personal connection with members of the press. This does not require you to invite them to lunch or remember their birthdays. (Nice if you do, though. And by the way, media generally pay for their own meals should you ask them out.) It is about knowing their areas of news and story interests and relating your expertise or research findings to their reporting. It is about developing a system of contact that works best for them.

In the *Washington Post* how-to guide about getting news into the paper editors advise, "Before faxing or e-mailing your news release, ask the person receiving the information how he or she prefers to receive the news. Reporters have different preferences—

some favor faxes or voicemail while others want releases via e-mail. Remember reporters are frequently reassigned so it is important you confirm the correct person is still covering the news you are sending."(1)

What those in the media do not like is to be on someone's mass mailing list and receive press releases that have little or nothing to do with their story interests. These missives are often about new faculty appointments or awards, conferences, presentations, grants received, and new programs that make no connection to the reporter's readers or viewers.

Because "News Release" is at the top of the page, that does not make it news, at least not in reporters' eyes. Resist the practice of blanketing media with press releases and hoping that something will stick. The only thing that usually does is creating a bad impression. Reporters, editors, and producers repeatedly tell me that they do not open letters and e-mails from institutions (major national universities in some cases) and individuals they feel waste their time by contacting them about non-news announcements or information that has nothing to do with their areas of coverage or their audience's interests.

Mistakes in contacting the media usually stem from not having a good sense about the person and outlet you are contacting and not being able to succinctly tell your story and explain why the reporter's readers, listeners, or viewers would be interested. Lacking a story, many people make pitches to the media out of frustration ("Why don't they write about us?"), fear ("My boss or my board is going to be angry that we're not in the story."), or ego ("I deserve to be in the article.").

The following are the "Top 10 Things You Should *Never* Say to the Media,"(2) according to Bad Pitch Blog, an online resource for PR professionals that asked readers to submit entries for this list of bad practices:

- This is a newly integrated solution that enables synergies and increases efficiencies between two previous incongruous applications.

- You should be interested in this because (the competition) covered it in their last issue.

- Did you get my: e-mail, voicemail, news release, press kit?

- You don't cover this beat? Can you forward it to the person who does?

- You'll be sorry tomorrow if you don't cover this news.

- I already pitched the *Wall Street Journal*, but they said no.

- We'll give you a local exclusive on this. The *Wall Street Journal* is doing a piece, but we don't view you as competitive.

- Since you didn't cover us after our last meeting, you really owe us a story.

- I saw an interesting piece on CNET and thought you'd be interested in doing a similar story.

Not on the list but a common complaint I often hear from reporters is about the person who calls shortly after a story appears. I label this the me-too pitch. The caller wants the reporter to know that his or her institution has a program similar to the one covered. The caller is hoping that lightning will strike twice, and that the reporter also will want to write about his or her initiative as well: "Seeing your article today about international education, I thought you might want to write about our study abroad program too." Writing about the same topic again in the short term does not keep reader interest, which is job number one for the reporter. To the journalist and his or her audience, news reported is no longer news.

Reporters need to move on. Their news beats, such as science, medicine, education, or foreign affairs, are generally broad in nature, and at best they can hope to cover only a small fraction of all that is newsworthy in their field. A caller pitching an installment to a story the reporter just wrote about (unless it is part of a series) will fall on deaf ears.

Being the same or a little different is not news. However, if the caller presented how his or her program as well as the one just reported plays in to a larger issue of possible news interest, the reporter might listen and welcome the discussion.

What Makes News

The essence of news is that it is of interest to readers, listeners, and viewers. If a news outlet wants to stay viable, there is no getting around this core principle. It is ingrained in every reporter, writer, editor, and producer, and no matter how hard you try, you will not get any of them to cover your story if they determine it would not be of interest to the wide range of people who read their papers or tune in to their broadcasts.

The truism coined over a century ago by John B. Bogart, said to be the best city editor in the country at the time, still holds: "When a dog bites a man, that is not news, because it happens so often. But if a man bites a dog, that is news."(3)

What is news to one media outlet, however, may not be to another. One national newspaper regularly reports the results of major surveys. Another generally does not. One magazine will report the weekly news events while another will interpret their larger meaning. One magazine regularly covers significant anniversary dates of major events (popular anniversary dates seem to be the 1st, 5th, 10th, 15th, 20th, and so on) while another does not because there is an anniversary of something every day. NPR tells listeners that the three key criteria it uses to determine whether a story airs on *All Things Considered* are that it needs to be "personal, brief, and have a twist."(4) Some reporters want stories that are counterintuitive, while others want the news to be surprising. One leading newspaper Web site is partial to stories that use numbers to support their results. This allows the site to use the "power of the Internet to show data," says its education editor. Other news Web sites have little or no original reporting and instead rely on news written by others.

Reporters often tell me their editors want more human interest stories, while others are looking for stories with artwork, such as graphs, charts, and photos. A *Chicago Tribune* editor tells his news staff to "enlighten, provoke, surprise and entertain" their readers.(5)

As for the types of stories that are of the most interest in a national magazine's education coverage, one editor said staff members are "looking for really counterintuitive, off-the-beaten-path type stuff concerning all aspects of undergraduate education. [They] also love stories that have to do with 'lists'—top 10 and so forth." An AP national reporter tells me that he "always is looking for the big story." Something that is "new and different and surprising."

News must be timely; the Internet demands it. News cycles of a daily newspaper are now blurred as reporters rush to immediately post news on the Web, let alone prepare stories for the next day's edition. News is being reported 24/7.

A call to a newspaper about a breaking story hours after the event can be too late. Opinion articles and letters to the editor commenting on a breaking news event are increasingly appearing in papers a day or two after the event has been reported. These pieces are being written as soon as the news appears and are instantly delivered by e-mail to the publication. Newspapers such as the *New York Times* and the *Wall Street Journal* have expanded their opinion pages on the Web, increasing the demand and turn-around time for article submissions. Traditional news cycles for the mainstream media once measured in days and weeks are gone.

In *Writing & Reporting the News*, authors and veteran journal-ists Gerald Lanson and Mitchell Stephens list 11 common criteria for evaluating newsworthiness of an event or issue.(6) Many pro-fessional journalists take these points into consideration, con-sciously or subconsciously, when considering if your story is news.

Impact. "The facts and events with the greatest impact on the most readers have the greatest news value."

Weight. The significance of the events as compared with others, for example, "loss of life has more weight than injury, and injuries generally are more newsworthy than loss of property."

Controversy. "The news loves arguments, debates, charges, coun-tercharges, and all-out fights."

Prominence. "Events in the lives of particularly well-known people . . . are given particular attention by the press."

The Unusual. "When a dog bites a man . . ." (see p. 28).

Proximity. "Readers are interested in the problems of people and places they know. All other things being equal, the closer the news is, the bigger it is."

Timeliness. "Most news that appears in daily newspapers happened either yesterday or today." On news Web sites, it often happened minutes ago.

Currency. "The news must also take into account what's on peo-ple's minds," for example, stories about holiday traditions are often popular around Thanksgiving.

Emotion. "Some news appeals directly to our emotions. Readers are not always concerned only with what is most important. Reporters must take into account these human interests."

Usefulness. "Readers regularly turn to their local newspaper [and other media] to help them solve problems and answer basic questions about their daily lives," for example, "news you can use."

Education Value. "[Make readers] more knowledgeable rather than merely informed. The better newspapers [and other media] today aren't merely telling that a space station is being built; they are discussing how it works."

"Two things that are not news," says former *Los Angeles Times* Washington deputy bureau chief and news editor Richard Cooper, are "One, something people already know. Two, things people did not know but would have assumed if they did" (dog bites man). "News," he says, "is something people don't know and wouldn't have assumed to be true." Other characteristics that Cooper believes make a story news: "News has to be new. Something people didn't know but would want to know. News affects the reader in an important way. It can be news because it is interesting."

CASE STUDY: USE SURVEYS

Surveys can begin discussions with the media where none existed before. By revealing new information on presumably important issues, surveys frequently generate strong media interest. Research center and policy institute directors and scholars have found that conveying the findings of their surveys opens doors for in-depth discussions about the issues central to their work.

The Community College Survey of Student Engagement (CCSSE), a counterpart to the NSSE, has used the findings of its annual survey to create a national dialogue about the goals, challenges, and value of the institutions it measures.

A constant effort of community colleges has been to create greater public understanding of the depth of their work and their critical importance to American higher education. (Most people, for example, may be unaware that over half of all college students in the United States are enrolled in community colleges.) Sometimes feeling like the Rodney Dangerfield of higher education, the comedian known for telling his audience, "I don't get no respect," community colleges traditionally have had a difficult time in getting the major media to care about them.

"It's a good story, but our readers don't attend community colleges," a *New York Times* education reporter once told me as he passed on an article idea I presented to him. The focus of the *Times*'s higher education reporting, as with the other major media, was on the highly selective private and top public four-year institutions, not community colleges, unless the news was bad.

CCSSE began to change this attitude and generate meaningful national media coverage about why the country should care about ensuring the health and success of community colleges. The survey gave a voice to community colleges, and the public was listening.

Survey director Kay McClenney used the annual results to create new dialogue with audiences important to community colleges, such as legislators, business leaders, educators, and the media. Each year the findings presented new information, which McClenney harnessed to tell her story about the state of community colleges and their vital role within the country's higher education system. The survey became a platform for major speeches, journal articles, opinion pieces, and national print, radio, and television interviews. The survey's success in capturing important new data, and McClenney's commitment to public outreach through the dissemination of findings and explaining their relevance, have led some who have closely followed the project to say with admirable recognition that CCSSE is not a survey but a change strategy.

A well-conducted, major, and meaningful survey is a powerful communication tool that can break down barriers to productive dialogue and understanding. It opens doors, sheds light on important issues, and gives the media the kind of information they can write about. Consider their use in your communications planning.

_____■

Notes

1. *Washington Post.* (November 2003). What's Your Story? A Guide for Getting News Into the Washington Post.

2. Dugan, K. (2007, November 13). *Top 10 Things You Should Never Say to the Media.* Retrieved from the Bad Pitch Blog: http://badpitch.blogs pot.com/2007/11/download-10-listen-too.html

3. *New York Times.* (1921, November 18). John B. Bogart Dies, Veteran Journalist. Retrieved December 31, 2009, from http://query.nytimes.com/gst/ abstract.html?res = 9800E7DE113CE533A2575BC1A9679 D946095D6CF

4. *All Things Considered.* (2008, April 25). What Makes a Story for NPR's *All Things Considered* (on-air promotion).

5. Romenesko, J. (2008, August 21). *Chicago Tribune's Goal: Get Readers Excited About the Paper.* Retrieved December 31, 2009, from Poynter-Online: http://www.poynter.org/column.asp?id = 45&aid = 149084

6. Lanson, G., & Stephens, M. (1994). *Writing & Reporting the News* (2nd ed.), pp. 10–15. New York: Oxford University Press.

CHAPTER FOUR

Developing a Media Strategy

PRIORITIZING THE MEDIA

This conversation is loaded with debate, and the Internet is changing the discussion as I write. Those in competing media outlets would disagree, but I believe that one of the best ways to get your story reported in depth with the greatest attention, particularly with high-level audiences such as legislators, business leaders, heads of major organizations and institutions, and with other media outlets, is to have it first appear in the *New York Times*. It is considered the newspaper of record, and the other major media refer to it as they set their own news agendas. Different media may do this for you as well, but when I have a choice on which media outlet to approach first with my story because the news that I am presenting is of major public importance or represents a significant national trend, the odds are the *Times* will deliver the readership and level of reporting I am seeking.

A story still floating around tells about the time during the early 1980s when the *New York Times* typesetters went on strike and the morning talk shows on the major television and radio networks were a little at a loss at first in determining their daily programming because a main source for news and story ideas had gone dark. The *Times*, then and now, influences much of the conversation in the mainstream media because of the financial resources it invests and the top reporters it hires to cover the news.

The Internet is changing this discussion, however, along with significant downsizing afoot in the news department at the *Times* and other traditional media outlets. A story appearing on a popular blog site today has the potential to have as much influence, or perhaps more, than a major newspaper. However, newspapers and other mainstream media are still the dominant source of news appearing on the Internet. A former *Los Angeles Times* editor studying Internet news coverage has estimated that 80% of all online news originates in print. Others, as one observer stated, believe it to be even higher: "As a longtime editor of an online journal who has taken part in hundreds of editorial meetings in which story ideas are generated from pieces that appeared in print, that figure [80%] strikes me as low."(1) In most cases, the traditional news outlets lead and the blogs follow on average by 2.5 hours, according to a Cornell University study of news cycles.(2) The research also showed that 3.5% of story lines that originated in blogs later appeared in the traditional media.

Story Placement

To generate the most coverage for your story, here is a framework for approaching the major media. It is not carved in stone, but I have found the most success in gaining the widest coverage when I contact the media based on the following criteria.

Major news wire services. Traditional and new media will run stories if they are important enough, such as the release of major new findings with significant public impact, and if they have first appeared on a major news wire service like the AP or Bloomberg News.

Major national newspapers. They compete with each other. The *New York Times* will not report a story that has first appeared in the *Wall Street Journal* and vice versa. This is mostly true but not always. Also, the major national dailies generally lead magazines and broadcasters in breaking stories. Internet news sites are primarily news aggregators, but the best, like slate.com and huffingtonpost.com, are increasingly breaking stories. The *New York Times* and other major newspapers are trying to figure out how to respond. Attitudes about not reporting on stories that have already appeared elsewhere seems begrudgingly to be changing.

Trying to justify not being first in reporting a story, one *Times* employee quipped in a conversation with me that if the *New York Times* hasn't reported it, the story hasn't been told.

The country's four major newspapers of record are the *New York Times*, *Wall Street Journal*, *Washington Post*, and *Los Angeles Times*.

Major weekly news magazines. These publications' print cycle keeps them for the most part from being first to report on breaking news. Their role is more to cover the major news of the past week and to provide analysis. Approaching these publications with a story that just appeared or is expected to soon run in a major newspaper does not threaten them. They would love to be the first to receive it, but since they are published weekly, a daily newspaper will break the news first. These news magazines also compete among themselves.

Major television and radio networks. Broadcast media rely on the major print news outlets for their story material. Broadcast outlets generally do not have the larger reporting staff the major print news organizations employ. Research is limited. However, they expect to air major stories the same day they appear in print. The hosts of morning talk shows fiercely compete among each other and will often demand exclusive interviews from their guests.

Internet news sites. Largely aggregators of news, Internet news sites rely on traditional media for their news postings. However, an increasing number of news sites are featuring original reporting. Salon.com and huffingtonpost.com offer staff-written news and features along with articles and blogs by guest contributors.

Scholarly journals and trade publications. Often the source of news and trends for mainstream media, these publications do not compete with popular media. They are a primary source for journalists in understanding the industries and fields of research they are reporting on. Your news that first appears in a scholarly or trade journal can be the best leverage you have in securing mainstream media's interest in your story. Journal and trade publication articles also better ensure accuracy of your story's future coverage by other media.

If you have a story that everyone wants, send it out at the same time to all the news outlets important to you and let them run with it. Don't worry about who competes with whom. If it is major breaking news, they all are likely to report on it. However, this type of news event is rare, and most stories need to be shopped around. Knowing how one media outlet responds to another is important as you try to generate the most coverage for your story. Having it first appear in a magazine may end your chances that it will appear in a national newspaper, whereas you may have had the opportunity to earn coverage in both. Remember, media relations is a science and an art. It is a combination of being creative in your approach and understanding the dynamics of news and how it is reported.

Offering an Exclusive

Offering an exclusive, meaning releasing your news to only one media outlet, can be a powerful incentive for a reporter or producer to tell your story. However, not all stories require providing an exclusive, and don't be quick to give it away. It is a strong bargaining chip between you and the media, and you don't want to play your hand too soon.

Offering a story exclusive can make the difference between your story being told or not. When exclusives are offered unnecessarily, the downside is that they are restricting, can limit your media coverage, and can make others in the media upset with you. The plus side is that your story may never be told unless you make it worth the reporter's time and effort by guaranteeing to the best of your ability that he or she gets to tell it first.

First, every reporter wants an exclusive and often will ask you for one when you are offering a story. Should you give it to the reporter? That depends. When it comes to major breaking news, such as the release of key findings from a major study with important public significance, these types of stories generally do not require exclusives and you should resist giving them. Mainstream media should have the option to report this news as soon as it is released. Though some would like to have an exclusive on breaking the story, this type of big news is too important not to be covered by the major media, even among the competing outlets.

However, for features and news with limited public appeal, offering an exclusive to a media outlet may help your story get off the ground. A particular reporter or producer may have an eye for your story that others in the media do not readily see and are not willing to invest time to develop. An added incentive is to make a promise, which is not to be broken, that this person will be the first to tell the story. In offering an exclusive, do not let it be open ended. Agree upon a timeline, and if the deadline passes and there is no story, be sure the reporter understands that you are free to contact other media.

An exclusive gives a reporter or producer some hope that other media outlets won't cover the story first. Herd journalism is real, and a huge motivator for the media to run a story is to hear that another news outlet plans to release it soon. One example of this is a university that repeatedly tried to interest the local bureau of a national newspaper in a new economic study by one of its professors. The story was continually met with a lack of interest from the bureau until its staff learned that the professor would be in New York later in the week to meet with major media organizations to discuss the study. Afraid of being scooped by the competition, the reporter at the local bureau raced to report the story, which prominently appeared on the front page of one of the paper's news sections a few days later. Giving an exclusive is meant to assure the reporter that you are not talking to other media about the story, increasing the odds that he or she will have time to report it and eliminate some of the worry that the competition might run it first.

If you need added leverage to interest a reporter in your story, offering an exclusive may be the course to take. You should have an honest sense about the public importance of your story before contacting the media, and you should understand the pros and cons of offering an exclusive. Be prepared for the reporter to ask for an exclusive, and know your answers ahead of time. Don't be caught by surprise and be too quick to give a response that you may regret later.

If you do give an exclusive to a reporter, don't break your promise even though a better media option later presents itself. There is a chance that you will offer an exclusive to one reporter, only to be contacted shortly afterward by another media outlet that is also interested in your story. Even if it's the *New York Times* calling, my advice is to stick with your promise. Your reputation is more valuable than breaking your word for the prospect of added coverage. Reneging on a promise is considered a mortal sin with the media, and you might find it hard to be forgiven. Also, if the news is that important, odds are other media will run the story after it first appears.

One of the worst media blunders comes from providing a reporter with an exclusive to a story that is released to other media outlets with an embargo date, meaning the news should not be released before that specific date. Sounds odd, but it happens. You will sometimes see this at press conferences. People from the media are invited to the event, and the news to be presented is embargoed until it's announced at the press conference. What happens, though, is that an aggressive reporter from a major media outlet will contact the newsmaker participating in the press conference and ask for the story early. The reporter then is given an exclusive and permission to run the story on the morning of the press conference. The newsmaker may see it as a slight transgression or just not understand the consequences, but the media attending the press conference who were told that the news is embargoed until the event will be furious when they read about it in the morning newspaper. You can bet they will take out their anger at the conference organizers, before the event, during, or later, and it is a position you do not want to be in. Whatever trust the event organizers might have built with the media is quickly lost and may be difficult, perhaps impossible, to regain.

This happened when a *New York Times* reporter contacted a college president prior to a press conference in New York City that the president was scheduled to participate in. Having received an invitation to attend and noting that the president was on the panel of speakers, the reporter asked the president to reveal the confidential details of the announcement that would be made public at the event. The president, whom I suspect thought he was making an important media friend, revealed the key news elements that would be released at the conference, and unbeknownst to the event organizer and other panel members, apparently gave the reporter an exclusive to run the story in the *Times* on the morning of the event. And the reporter did.

Angry people from the media filled the room, with a copy of the *Times* in hand. "Why did you give the *Times* the story first?" yelled one reporter to the panel members who were caught by surprise, except for one. "Why did you make us honor the embargo, but not the *Times*?" another reporter demanded to know. Major news outlets that planned to cover the story did not. The event organizers and their participants stammered to find answers. The good faith that had been built between the media and the sponsors of the event was lost, and it took a lot of time before the media wanted to hear from them again.

The irony with the president's giving an exclusive and allowing the *Times* to break the embargo is that had he not agreed, the *Times* reporter probably would have still attended the event and reported on it along with the other media since the news was significant.

Notes

1. Kamiya, G. (2009, February 17). *The Death of the News*. Retrieved February 19, 2009, from Salon: http://www.salon.com/opinion/kamiya/2009/02/17/newspapers/

2. Lohr, S. (2009, July 13). Study Measures the Chatter of the News Cycle. Retrieved July 14, 2009, from the *New York Times*: http://www.nytimes.com/2009/07/13/technology/internet/13influence.html?_r = 1&sq = steve . . .

CHAPTER FIVE

Presenting Your Story in Writing

As there is no shortage of story ideas sent regularly to the major media outlets, when you send a story proposal to the media, it pretty much lives or dies based on what is presented in the first sentence or two. When presenting your story to reporters, editors, and producers, you need to tell them up front what is most important in your letter, e-mail, or news release. In other words, why should their readers or viewers care?

Words that often grab attention in a story are *first*, *discovery*, *new finding*, *breakthrough*, and the most of something: *largest*, *tallest*, *heaviest*, *smallest*, and so on. These words are factual, objective, and can be substantiated. They have real meaning.

This writing style is called the inverted pyramid, "in which the top is heavy with important facts and trails off into less significant information," noted the *New York Times*.(1) "Ease of reading becomes a requisite. Clarity is essential," George Fox wrote in his primer for journalists, *New Survey of Journalism*.(2)

The foundation for news reporting is presenting the who, what, where, when, why, and how of a story. Add to this the three Cs: clear, concise, and correct.

Your letter, e-mail, or news release will benefit by following these writing guidelines that journalists strive to perfect.

The following is the lead paragraph of a news release from the University of Virginia that follows traditional news reporting form. Note how all the important facts are clearly and concisely presented, answering in the first few sentences the five Ws and H that reporters and editors are sure to ask.

> April 10, 2008—Air pollution from power plants and automobiles is destroying the fragrance of flowers and thereby inhibiting the ability of pollinating insects to follow scent trails to their sources, a new University of Virginia study indicates. This could partially explain why wild populations of some pollinators, particularly bees—which need nectar for food—are declining in several areas of the world, including California and the Netherlands.(3)

Who is the University of Virginia.

What is a new study about environmental factors that affect the behavior of pollinating insects.

Where is several areas of the world, including California and the Netherlands.

When is the present.

Why is because the fragrance of flowers is being destroyed.

How is from air pollution from power plants and automobiles.

Rudyard Kipling helps us try to remember the five Ws and *H* in the first lines of his 1902 poem "I keep six honest serving-men":

> I keep six honest serving-men
> (They taught me all I knew);
> Their names are What and Why and When
> And How and Where and Who.(4)

Another formula that journalists follow in telling a story is Hey, You, See, and So.

Bob Dotson, NBC correspondent whose "American Story" segments appear on the *Today* show said that every broadcast story should include these elements:

> "Hey," give me your attention.
>
> "You" is the reason why you should care about this story wherever you are.
>
> "See" is the two or three facts you have in your story that nobody else knows.
>
> "So" is why the viewer should care.(5)

With regard to good writing, Roy Peter Clark, a well-known writing teacher for journalists and the author of many books on effective writing, offers this advice about empowering the subject and the verb when telling your story: "The creation of meaning—expression of a complete thought—requires a subject and a verb, the king and queen of comprehensibility. And the king and queen are most powerful when they sit on thrones besides each other rather than in separate castles far away."(6)

One example he gives is a lead to a story that appeared in the *New York Times*.

> Gov. Eliot Spitzer, whose rise to political power as a fierce enforcer of ethics in public life was undone by revelations of his own involvement with prostitutes, resigned on Wednesday, becoming the first New York governor to leave office amid scandal in nearly a century."(7)

Shortening the distance between the subject and the verb, Clark offers this rewrite, which he believes makes the story more comprehensible.

Gov. Eliot Spitzer resigned on Wednesday, becoming the first New York governor in nearly a century to leave office amid scandal. Having risen to power as a fierce enforcer of ethics in public life, Spitzer was undone by revelations of his own involvement with prostitutes.

Adopt media's style of writing when presenting your story. Reporters, editors, and producers will welcome your effort, and your story will have a better chance of being noticed by them if you follow the basic journalistic guidelines for writing.

Press Release

When announcing major events, new research findings, or dealing with a crisis, a press release can best present your information in a clear, concise, and compelling manner. The following are basic guidelines for writing a press release:

- ◆ Use standard 8 1/2 × 11 inch white paper, double space, and wide margins.

- ◆ Use only one side of the page. If the release runs more than one page, type the word "more" at the bottom of each page, except the last one. Try to keep your release to two pages or less (many would argue no more than one; use your judgment). Use page numbers. At the end of the release, type the journalistic mark -30- or ###, which signifies the end. Staple multiple pages.

- ◆ Note contact information at the top of the first page: name, title, institution, essential phone numbers (day and evening), and e-mail address.

♦ Note the release date at the top of the first page, for example, For Immediate Release, or Embargoed for Release November 15, 20–.

♦ Give your release a headline that provides the reader (i.e., a busy reporter or editor with no time to spare) a quick sense of the story: "New Research Shows . . ."

♦ Include photos or graphics that add to your story. Good visuals can increase the odds of a story's being reported.

♦ Add Web links that provide more information (see the sample release on pp. 51–54).

Press or news releases, whether presented on paper or electronically, have their limitations. They do a good job of presenting timely information in a succinct fashion, but they rarely sell a story, as many reporters and editors from major media outlets might tell you. Allen Hammond, former editor of the defunct journal *Science 80–86*, revealed in an interview long ago that a news release had about "a one-thousandth chance of getting into his magazine."(8) After all the years that have passed since offering this insight, Hammond might say that today the odds against a press release resulting in coverage in any major publication are even higher because of greater competition for news space. Newsrooms are flooded with press releases day and night. No longer do these missives come just in the morning's mail, as they did in Hammond's day. Newsrooms are bombarded with news releases around the clock. More than once I've watched faxes as they poured into the *New York Times* newsroom, falling to the floor in small mountains and streams of unread releases. Snail mail, overnight express, faxes, and e-mail have all been co-opted to deliver information that for the most part has little or no news value to the reporter. People from national media organizations tell me they still receive press releases from major universities to little-known colleges about faculty appointments, fund-raising events, awards, and other non-news items that have no chance of making it into their publications or on the air.

Why do people send them? Lack of news judgment is one reason. Another is, like junk mail, which news releases are often considered to be by the media, the sender hopes that somebody, somewhere will respond. News releases may be a convenient tool for the sender attempting to reach reporters, editors, and producers, but if they lack news value, sending them is a negative exercise that can detract from one's reputation rather than add to it.

Not all press releases are misplaced. When news needs to get out right away, they are an effective instrument to deliver your message. Show restraint, though, in sending them far and wide when the news may be more for a local audience. Resist using mass mailing lists, which inherently suffer from being outdated. When it comes to contacting media: Target, target, target.

E-Mail

What worked for Allen Hammond, and still does today with the media in general, is to send a targeted query letter presenting your story idea. Explain in the first few sentences why you believe your story is important and why the reporter's audience would care. "About 40 percent of our articles arise from ideas that come in through query letters," Hammond said. For him, it showed "that somebody thought about this magazine and decided this story was right for us."(9)

A targeted e-mail is often how reporters want to be contacted about story ideas. However, this was not always true. In the beginning of e-mail technology, many reporters, as others, held their e-mail addresses as sacred. It was considered a breach of privacy if someone from the public would send them an e-mail without first asking permission. The annoyance level for reporters receiving unsolicited e-mail was comparable to receiving a sales call at home during dinner. For the most part, this has changed. Many reporters now list their e-mail address at the end of their stories. When a story idea is concise and targeted, reporters appreciate the speed, clarity, and the option for more information via embedded Web links that e-mail can provide.

At its core, an effective e-mail to a reporter follows the same writing principles of a news release (it includes the five Ws and H), but uses fewer words. It often may be no longer than a brief paragraph or two. It is personal: "Dear Mr. or Ms." It recognizes the reporter's story interest: "Following your reporting about climate change." It gets to the point: "I am writing to introduce new research that will be released next month about the polar ice melt. The findings should have a major impact on global CO_2 emissions guidelines." It provides options for more information: "Enclosed are links that offer added background." It suggests a follow-up: "I would like to give you a call to discuss this new study."

The reporter has the option to respond or wait for a follow-up call. Most people don't like making these story calls to members of the media (after nearly 30 years in media relations, I still pause before I pick up the phone), but I have found them to be essential in the process of generating media coverage. And your e-mail may not have been delivered to the reporter because it was blocked by ever more aggressive e-mail filters. Your follow-up call to provide added story background will verify whether your original information was received.

■
CASE STUDY: KEEP IT SIMPLE

You have so much to say, and the issues are complicated. Your message can't be told in sound bites, and you are not going to dumb down the conversation. Many of the most complicated stories, however, can be told using the simplest terms and examples that, contrary to dumbing down the discussion, elevate it. The use of concise, unburdened language and meaningful metaphors can bring a conversation alive and reach new audiences. Conversations and storytelling burdened with the jargon of one's profession or discipline pushes away people who are outside the field, and sometimes those within.

Think of all we learn when reading a well-written article in the *The Economist* or the *Los Angeles Times* on an issue we are unfamiliar with, say, microfinancing in third world countries. We appreciate that the reporter and the people interviewed in the article told the story in a way that made it accessible and informative for us, the general reader. We learned something we did not know before, and it may prompt us to want to learn more.

Patrick Callan, president of the National Center for Public Policy and Higher Education, understands the importance of presenting messages in clear, concise terms, as he does with his center's 50-state report card on higher education. The eloquence of the model, a report that gives states letter grades (A, B, C, D, F) and "incompletes" based on their performance in delivering higher education to their residents, took a conversation historically buried in data and confusion and brought it alive. Now taxpayers, legislators, and educators could work off the same page to bring about meaningful change.

The report card is an exemplar of two important communications and marketing principals: Keep it simple (KIS) and Create attention, interest, desire, and action (AIDA) in building your story (AIDA is discussed in greater detail in chapter 7). This biennial letter-grade report, titled *Measuring Up*, has received extensive news coverage by local, state, and national media. The *New York Times*, *Washington Post*, *Los Angeles Times*, *Wall Street Journal*, *Time*, AP, *PBS NewsHour*, NPR, and a number of other media outlets have reported on it. It has become a major point of reference in knowledge-based discussions about bringing about needed change in the performance of states to provide high-quality and affordable higher education.

The center's *Measuring Up* used words, graphs, and charts that brought the public into the conversation. It took the time to be concise and demonstrated concern and respect for its audiences. Information was not dumbed down but elevated by its clarity. One national foundation president referred to the center's use of a report card to convey complicated data as brilliant. Don't be afraid to keep it simple in telling your story. It will let more people know of your intelligence and the important information you have to present.

Here is a sample of a National Center press release for *Measuring Up*.

The National Center for Public Policy and Higher Education

EMBARGOED FOR RELEASE:	Contact:
September 7, 2006	Daphne Borromeo
	408-271-2699
	dborromeo@higher
	education.org

State News Summary: Virginia
Virginia Performs Well in Preparing Students
for College, but Lags in Making Higher Education Affordable

San Jose, CA, and Washington, D.C.—Virginia compares well with most other states in preparing students for college, but higher education in Virginia has become less affordable for students and their families since the early 1990s. In addition, young adults from high-income families are about four times as likely as those from low-income families to attend college. If these trends are not addressed, they could undermine the state's access to an educated, competitive workforce and weaken its economy over time.

These are among the major findings of *Measuring Up 2006: The National Report Card on Higher Education* released today by the independent, nonpartisan National Center for Public Policy and Higher Education. According to the report:

♦ Eighth graders in Virginia perform well on national assessments in math, science, and reading. Over the past nine years, 8th graders' performance on national science assessments has improved substantially (28%), exceeding the nationwide increase on this measure (1%).

♦ Net college costs for students from low- and middle-income families to attend community colleges—the least expensive colleges in the state—represent about one-third of their annual family income. (Net college costs equal tuition, room, and board after financial aid.) For these students at public four-year colleges and universities, net college costs represent 41% of their annual family income. These two sectors enroll 82% of the state's college students.

♦ Among young adults (ages 18–24), there are still substantial gaps in college participation between whites and non-whites. Currently, 40 out of 100 white young adults are enrolled in college, compared with 25 out of 100 young adults from other ethnic groups.

♦ In addition, young adults from high-income families are about four times as likely as those from low-income families to attend college—the widest gap in the nation on this measure.

♦ Virginia lags many countries in the proportion of students who complete certificates or degrees. With 16 out of 100 students enrolled completing certificates or degrees, the state lags countries such as Poland, the Slovak Republic, and Portugal.

"Our future educational and economic leadership is in jeopardy if the nation's young population—those already in the workforce and those still in the educational pipeline—do not keep pace with the levels of college access and completion of earlier generations and with the accelerating pace of college education throughout the world," said Patrick Callan, president of the National Center. "*Measuring Up 2006* provides state policymakers and higher education leaders with a clear understanding of where postsecondary education needs to improve in their state."

The grades in the report card are based on quantitative measures; each state is graded on six areas of performance. For the first time, this edition of *Measuring Up* includes international comparisons for each of the 50 states and the United States as a whole on their performance in providing postsecondary education.

Forty-one states received an "Incomplete" in Learning, a category that evaluates what is known about student learning as a result of education and training beyond high school. For these states, it is not possible to measure the state's educational capital—the reservoir of high-level knowledge and skills that benefit each state—due to inadequate data.

VIRGINIA'S GRADES

Preparation   A –

Participation	B
Affordability	F
Completion	B+
Benefits	A
Learning	Incomplete

Measuring Up 2006 includes a national report and 50 state reports. The national report summarizes the nation's current performance in higher education, as well as improvements or declines in performance over the past decade. The individual state reports offer a detailed look at higher education in each state. *Measuring Up 2006* follows up on previous editions of the report card released in 2000, 2002, and 2004.

Upon the release of *Measuring Up 2006* on September 7, the national and state reports will be available on the National Center's Web site at www.highereducation.org. The Web site also offers state-by-state comparisons and information about the methodology used in *Measuring Up 2006*.

The National Center for Public Policy and Higher Education promotes policies that enhance Americans' opportunities to pursue and achieve a quality higher education. Established in 1998, the National Center is an independent, nonprofit, nonpartisan organization. It is not associated with any institution of higher education, with any political party, or with any government agency. ∎

Notes

1. Glaberson, W. (1993, April 2). Newspapers Told: Simplify, Simplify. Retrieved December 31, 2009, from the *New York Times*: http://www .nytimes.com/1993/04/02/us/newspapers-told-simplify-simplify.html?scp = 1& sq = william%20glaberson%20newspapers%20told%20simplify&st = cse

2. Mott, G. F., and others (Eds.) (1958). The word pattern of news. In *New Survey of Journalism* (4th ed.), pp. 49–56, Barnes & Noble.

3. Samarrai, F. (2008, April 10). *Flowers' Fragrance Diminished by Air Pollution, University of Virginia Study Indicates.* Retrieved November 17, 2009, from the University of Virginia: http://news.clas.virginia.edu/biology/x13264.xml?

4. Kipling, R. (1900, April). *The Elephant's Child.* Retrieved November 27, 2009, from the Kipling Society: http://www.kipling.org.uk/rg_elephants child1.htm

5. Tompkins, A. (2007, July 2). *Monday Edition: Bob Dotson's Essential Storytelling Tools.* Retrieved November 27, 2009, from Poynter Online: http://www.poynter.org/column.asp?id = 2&aid = 125933&view = . . .

6. Clark, R. P. (2008, August 14). *Branching Out Can Leave Verbs Out on a Limb.* Retrieved November 27, 2009, from Poynter Online: http://www.poynter.org/column.asp?id = 78&aid = 148598&view . . .

7. Grynbaum, M. (2008, March 12). Spitzer Resigns, Citing Personal Failings. Retrieved December 31, 2009, from the *New York Times*: http://www.nytimes.com/2008/03/12/nyregion/12cnd-resign.html?scp = 1&sq = spitzer%20resigns%20citing%20personal%20failings&st = cse

8. Peterson, G. (1982, February). *How to place science stories*, p. 3. CASE Answer File. Selected how-to articles from CASE CURRENTS.

9. Peterson, CASE Answer File.

CHAPTER SIX

Calling the Media

If you are serious about wanting to generate media coverage for an issue, study, or program important to you, the key to the job is being prepared to pick up the phone and talk with a reporter or a producer.

Even media relations specialists (usually the less-successful ones) try to avoid making telephone calls to the media. They argue that reporters, editors, and producers don't want to be bothered with calls and the stories they've presented in writing to them should stand on their own. In a perfect world this could be true, but when some reporters, editors, and producers receive nearly a hundred or more unsolicited e-mails a day, breaking through the clutter with a well-placed phone call can bring a story to their attention. Keep in mind too that those in the media make calls all the time to establish new contacts for their stories. It is how news is covered. The key is being smart about making the call.

I find in general that the best time to call major media outlets is between 10:30 a.m. and 3:00 p.m. Reporters and editors in New York and Washington, for example, often arrive at their offices between 9:00 and 10:00 in the morning and work at their desks until 6:00 or 7:00 in the evening on an average day. For morning papers, the crunch time for reporters is in the late afternoon and early evening as they write their stories for the next day's edition. For newspapers that appear in the afternoon, reporters are busiest during the morning and early afternoon hours as they race to meet story deadlines.

The 10:30 a.m. to 3:00 p.m. daily calling window also applies to many of the weekly national magazines. It is also good to know which day of the week the magazine "goes to bed," the weekly closing day for all stories to be turned in by reporters before the magazine goes to press. This generally is not a good time to call. Some of the major newsweeklies like *Newsweek* close on Fridays. Others, such as *Business Week*, close on Wednesdays.

Television and radio vary even more as far as the best times to contact a reporter or producer. If a broadcast airs at 4:00 in the afternoon, calling an hour before show time probably will connect you to a voice on an answering machine asking you to leave a message. Or you may get a live, harried reporter or producer who tells you, politely or not, that it is a bad time to talk.

The rule about deadlines and best times to talk with someone in the media is to ask the person you are calling. For each reporter, editor, and producer it can be different. Remember too that reporters for Internet Web sites also have multiple deadlines as they write news to post on the Web throughout the day.

What to Say When You Call

When I call a reporter, I introduce myself; briefly note why I am calling, for example, following up on an e-mail I sent about a new report soon to be released; and then ask if it is a good time to take a few minutes to discuss it. If it is not, I ask if there is a good time to call back. And if the person is not interested in the story, I ask if there is another reporter who might be. I spare the reporter the hard sell and present the story based on its interesting facts and timeliness. I get to the point right from the start, answering the questions the reporter most likely wants answered. The biggest being: Why is it a story? and Why should my readers (viewers or listeners) care? If you can't answer these questions and present your information in a concise and compelling way, don't make the call.

It is important in presenting a story to the media to avoid using loose terms to define your work. Too often a professor will tell me about his or her unique program, only for me to learn later with a little investigation that other colleges and universities have similar initiatives. One professor told me his program was unique and only three other schools were doing it! Choose your words carefully when presenting your story. Making the news is not about spin. Standards for accuracy in the media are no less than what your profession demands. Media professionals need facts, and they are quick to unmask exaggerated statements. Do not give them reason to doubt what you are telling them. Once they do, you risk losing them. Enthusiasm is important, but spare the hyperbole.

Also, avoid calling a reporter only to ask, "Did you receive my story?" These kinds of calls are counterproductive, and those in the media find them annoying. Calls to the media should be about presenting new information and ideas. If you are following up on an earlier correspondence, be ready to offer additional information that further builds on your story. Remember, media professionals hate to have their time wasted, as do we all.

Three *Washington Post* science reporters wrote a letter a number of years ago to the National Association of Science Writers newsletter offering advice to people who contact them about a story idea. The following advice is timeless and can be applied to all media:

1. We appreciate an occasional phone call on a story of truly great importance—we don't always have time to scan our mail.

2. We don't need or appreciate calls to say "Did you get our press kit" on the umpteenth new beta blocker or energy-conversion device.

3. In spite of previous pleas, we are getting an increasing, not decreasing, flood of mail from the PR people of associations, universities, PR firms and drug companies. Some are sending us multiple mailings weekly. Some send us the latest vice presidential appointments. Many send us story after story they must know do not have the remotest chance of being printed.

Let all the guilty know that all envelopes [and e-mail] bearing their names are generally going into the wastebasket unopened— not because we're mean but because we've found the payoff from them is so small when we're confronted with stacks of new mail daily.(1)

Whom to Contact

When approaching media outlets about a story idea, several people can be contacted within the organization. For print, it could be a researcher, reporter, writer, correspondent, columnist, editorial board member, managing editor, or editor. For broadcast, it could be a researcher, booking agent (booker), correspondent, editor, segment producer, or producer. In some cases, it could also be a combination of individuals.

I generally find the best initial contact is the person who would have the most responsibility in writing or producing the story I am presenting. For print media, it is often the reporter or writer, and for broadcast it is the segment producer. Each outlet varies, however, and it may take a call or two to find out whom to approach with your story.

I start by contacting the reporter covering the field that best fits my story. Common news beats for most news media include business, medicine, health, science, technology, arts, culture, sports, education, and politics. Also there are metro, national, and foreign news desks. For example, for important changes in a college curriculum I'll contact the higher education reporter at a media outlet of interest to me. I often know the name of the reporter covering a news beat because I have been following his or her coverage. If I don't have a name, and it is a publication, I'll review the masthead, which generally lists the publisher, editorial board, and sometimes the news staff along with their areas of reporting, and is often located at the beginning or end of a newspaper or magazine or on its editorial page.

For print and broadcast, I have found that more detailed information about news and production staff assignments is often provided on the outlet's Web site under its contact information link. The *Chronicle of Higher Education*, for example, does an excellent job of listing each member of its news staff along with his or her area of coverage, telephone number, and e-mail address. *USA Today* provides a Reporter Index page on its Web site that lists reporters alphabetically along with links to stories they have written. Some listings also include links to profiles of the reporters. I also conduct a key word search on the outlet's Web site for the topic of interest to me as it relates to my story and to see who is writing about it.

If I am still uncertain whom to contact, I will call the main telephone number of the news outlet and ask for the name of the reporter or segment producer covering a specific beat. If the operator doesn't know or is uncertain, which often happens, I'll ask to be transferred to the specific news desk, for example, national politics, or the programming department for a particular show. At this point, I am often connected to a reporter or production staff member.

Reporters and producers may not enjoy taking these kinds of information-gathering calls, but I have generally found they understand the honesty of the query and realize the legitimacy of the request, particularly if the outlet does not post this information in its publication or on its Web site. Many times in these situations the person I am speaking to asks what the story is and this leads to a discussion or obtains the person's interest.

Sometimes I'll have a story that may not fit one particular news beat but fits a combination of beats. It might be a science and business story, for example. Also, a switchboard operator or a reporter on the news desk may not readily know who the best person is to contact about a particular story. In these cases, I'll ask to talk to an editor for a specific topic such as science or for a news desk that I think best fits my story, such as local, national, or international. Getting right to the point, I'll present the news highlights of my story and ask the editor who the best person is for me to approach. Usually, I receive a cordial and thoughtful response along with a recommended name. Sometimes it may be the editor I'm on the phone with or a reporter suggested by the editor, whose name I'll mention in my follow-up correspondence or conversation to the reporter.

Targeting your story to the right reporter, editor, or producer is essential in the process of generating media coverage. Why go to all the effort of developing a story and then send it to the wrong person? Yet many people do. Reporters, editors, and producers constantly complain, and rightly so, about receiving poorly targeted stories that have little or no relevance to them. "Take me off your mailing list" is a common refrain from media who receive an endless number of releases that have little or no importance to them.

"No harm in trying," say some people who are attempting to gain the media's interest. However, there is when care is not taken. Those in the media remember individuals and institutions that waste their time with poorly crafted stories or with news and ideas not targeted to their areas of coverage. Quickly their letters, e-mails, and telephone calls go unopened and unanswered, and their reputations suffer.

On the other hand, the business of media professionals is reporting the news, and if you have a good story let them know. They will be glad to hear from you.

Titles and Functions

The following is a brief list of job titles and the functions of the position:

Editors assign stories and give deadlines to reporters and writers. They review story content for clarity and accuracy.

Reporters and writers gather information and write news stories. Sometimes *reporter* and *writer* are synonymous within a news organization. When a reporter and writer are assigned to a story, one is primarily responsible for gathering information while the other writes the finished article.

Producers are active in all aspects of a broadcast production from beginning to end, including the creative, technological, financial, and administrative tasks.

Segment producers are responsible for one or more segments of a multisegment production; for example, there is a medical segment producer for ABC's *Good Morning America*. They also schedule guests and prepare interview questions for on-air talent.

Bookers develop story ideas, recommend guests, pitch ideas to producers, pre-interview guests, and coordinate their broadcast appearance.

In an interview on FlowTV, an online critical forum on television and media culture, Sara Leeder, a segment producer for CNBC, described her job responsibilities as follows:

> I book guests, pitch story ideas (we have a daily meeting), prepare [the host] with a research book for every segment, pre-interview each guest over the phone, write suggested questions, work with [the host] to select which questions we'll use, and edit the interview after it's taped.(2)

According to CNN, "A booker creates a story and guest ideas, pitches them to other staff members like the executive producer and the host, and then tracks the guests down—talks them into being on the show. The booker then writes interview questions, researches the topic and the guest, and then works with satellites to beam the guest in live for their show appearance."(3)

News positions and the responsibilities assigned to them are different for each news outlet. When in doubt, ask. One of the keys to media success is presenting your story to the right person.

Notes

1. Cohn, V., Hilts, P., & Russell, C. "Personal plea." Letter to the Editor. *National Association of Science Writers Newsletter.*

2. Griffin, H. (2005, February 4). *Interview with Sara Leeder, Segment Producer for CNBC's "Topic [A] with Tina Brown.* Retrieved from FLOW TV: http://flowtv.org/?p = 784

3. *Behind the Scenes at CNN.* Retrieved August 9, 2008, from http://www.cox.com/education/cnn/goldman.asp

CHAPTER SEVEN

Media Sessions

There is no shortage of good story ideas for the media to report. Each day brings more choices. The challenge for many reporters and producers is which story to cover next, and the decision may come down to whomever last caught their attention.

More than a letter, e-mail, or phone call, sitting down with a reporter, editor, or producer and having a face-to-face conversation about an important story idea offers one of the strongest ways to earn and keep the media's attention. Your story, if it has merit, can rise to the top of the list because of the timeliness and depth of the information you've presented in your conversation.

A media session, or deskside briefing as it is also called, by no means guarantees coverage, but it can be a valuable step in presenting your story and gaining interest in it.

Your visit gets those in the media to step aside from their usually hectic day and focus on you and your story. Your passion for the issues also drives home the importance of the discussion. All these factors, plus the fact that your contact has invested probably an hour in the discussion, increase the odds of generating interest in your ideas.

Media sessions also can develop trust between you and the journalist, and it can begin a mutually beneficial long-term professional relationship. This became particularly apparent to me when I met with a science reporter during a trip to Los Angeles. Staff members from the colleges and universities in the area whom I knew had interactions with this reporter found him to be gruff and difficult to work with. He was impatient and gave the impression that the last thing he wanted was to talk with anyone who wasn't part of a story he was reporting at the time. "Don't call me, I'll call you," might have been a fitting inscription for a sign on his desk.

I had worked with this reporter over the years, presenting story ideas from our client colleges and universities and providing experts from our campuses when he called for story sources. During my visit to L.A., I wanted to say hello and put a face behind the voice as well as learn more about his story interests. When we met in his office, I asked where he finds his story sources. He answered, "I call on the people who take the time to meet with me." I was pleasantly surprised that this apparently "tough character," as some had made him out to be, was actually very open to meeting with people who reached out to him to introduce their expertise as it related to his areas of reporting.

Journalists are not immune to common courtesies. Dale Carnegie recognized shared values and needs common among us all in his landmark people-skills book, *How to Win Friends and Influence People*. "Become genuinely interested in other people," and "Talk in terms of the other person's interests," he advised.(1) These skills can serve us well in all personal interaction and, very specifically, lend themselves to effectively dealing with the media. And, if Carnegie had been a journalist offering advice on working with media, he might have added, "Don't waste a reporter's time," and "Know the reporter's area of coverage and why your story would be of interest to his or her readers, listeners, or viewers."

Setting up a media session is like arranging any other business meeting: There is a defined purpose that should be mutually beneficial to both parties. For many scholars and researchers who have gone through the process, it can be similar to arranging a meeting with a funding agency to present a project and solicit support.

Before you pick up the phone or send an e-mail asking to get together, you need to be familiar with the journalist's reporting and be able to concisely relate your expertise to his or her area of interest. You should offer new information of news value, and a meeting allows the opportunity to explore this in more depth.

Having established the news importance of your expertise, the reason for the meeting can be as simple as your being in town and wanting to take the opportunity to introduce yourself in person. It may be that you are in the area to attend a major conference, or even better, you will be presenting a paper that relates to the reporter's area of interest, thus adding to the timeliness and importance of getting together.

Here is how a call to a reporter, editor, or producer might sound:

> *Caller*: "Ms. Rogers, my name is Bill Jones. I am a professor of politics at Best University and my focus of research is the presidential election process. I am calling about concerns regarding the Electoral College. Is this a good time to talk to you for a couple of minutes?"
>
> *Reporter*: "Yes, I have a few minutes. How can I help you?"
>
> *Caller*: "I've been following your coverage of this year's election, and based on my research, I am concerned that there is a possibility there could be a tie vote within the Electoral College."
>
> *Reporter*: "Interesting."
>
> *Caller*: "I'll be in Washington at the end of this month to attend a conference of scholars on the presidential election, and I am calling to see if you would be interested to meet and discuss this issue of the Electoral College and related matters concerning this

year's campaign. I'll be delivering a paper on the topic at the conference, and I can share this with you should we meet."

Reporter: "Sure. What time would you like to get together?"

Don't be frustrated, however, if a reporter does not want to or cannot meet. There can be a lot of good reasons, but it doesn't have to mean that the reporter didn't appreciate your asking. Also, don't let it stop you from contacting other reporters at other media outlets about getting together. Because of reporters' conflicting schedules and competing story interests at the time, I might call four, five, or six reporters before securing an appointment. All of these calls, though, I believe have value. They allow me to make personal contact with reporters of interest to me and to introduce and discuss my story. There is a good chance too that they create opportunities to send follow-up information. It also is not unusual for a reporter to offer a rain check to meet the next time you are in town.

I generally call about two to three weeks in advance to schedule an appointment. A reporter, editor, or producer often does not want to commit to a meeting too far ahead because he or she needs to stay available to cover breaking news. Also, if your schedule allows, try to be flexible about selecting a time to meet. Be ready to offer an alternative time or day to get together.

A meeting runs about an hour in length and is generally conducted in the reporter's office. If you are the one initiating the meeting, don't ask the reporter to meet you at your hotel unless he or she offers. You are the one asking for the reporter's time, and you should make getting together convenient for him or her.

A media session has two important stages: first is meeting with the reporter, second is the follow-up. Think of it in terms of the marketing principle, AIDA (attention, interest, desire, and action). The media session gets a reporter's attention for your story and ideally builds his or her interest (the reporter sees the news value of what you are presenting) and desire (the reporter sees it could be of interest to his or her readers or viewers). This is a lot to accomplish in a meeting that generally runs about an hour, but it is the foundation for continuing the discussion. The final step is action, getting the reporter to move on your story.

Remember, there is no shortage of good story ideas, and although a reporter expressed interest in what you had to say during your meeting, you need to get him or her to act upon it. News is breaking around the clock, and stories continually compete for a reporter's attention. Keeping your story front and center in the reporter's mind comes from follow-up.

Effective follow-up provides more information that further builds your story. It links to new developments that lend to the timeliness of the story, such as the release of a report, an upcoming legislative hearing, or passage of a new bill. It may offer added expert sources who can provide further insight to the discussion, or it can be a news article that highlights the urgency of your story.

Make every follow-up to a reporter important by providing added story information. Don't take up a reporter's time with telephone calls and e-mails that only ask if he or she is still interested in your story. This can eventually turn the reporter away. There is a fine line between meaningful follow-up and becoming tiresome to the reporter. Make your contact productive. Provide the reporter with the kind of information that makes the story hard to resist because you have made available just about everything he or she needs to report it. It is not the reporter's job to tell your story, just as it is not a foundation's job to give you money for a project. You have to earn what you want in each case.

Note

1. Carnegie, D. (1936). *How to Win Friends and Influence People*, p. 103. New York: Simon & Schuster.

CHAPTER EIGHT

Resources for Contacting the Media

The news business is fluid, and reporters' beats change regularly. You may have known a reporter who covered education for years only to find that this person is on the foreign affairs news desk now. Fortunately, there are ways to keep up with the constantly changing world of reporting the news.

Media Directories and Newsstands

A good place to start in identifying the media you would like to contact is to look through a media resource guide such as the *News Media Yellow Book*, *Bacon's Media Directories*, Burrelles-Luce Media Contacts, and others that provide information to paying subscribers. These references, many of which are available in print and online, list media by the type of news organization, for example, news services, newspapers, television, magazines, televisions, and radio programs; geographical location; and subject, for example, education, health, politics. Editors, producers, writers, and reporters are identified, and their titles are listed along with contact information. These directories can be expensive for an individual user, so check with your institution's public relations office or library to see if it can provide this resource to you.

You may find that a more personal and enjoyable way to identify print media and contacts is to head to a book store or newsstand and peruse the magazine and newspaper sections. Purchase what you like for a more thorough study or take notes, jotting down the contact information for the publication along with the names of writers of interest. You should be able to find more information later on the publication's Web site.

Institutional Support

If you are affiliated with a college or university, most likely the office of public relations, public affairs, or communications has media relations specialists on staff. Introduce yourself to them. Let them know about your interest in media coverage, possibly serving as an expert source on a timely topic or for a new project or research that you believe to have news value. They should welcome the visit and meet with you to discuss your media options and if warranted develop a plan. Remember, the media relations staff is only as effective as the strength of your story. They cannot generate coverage for you when your story is not news. Trust in their news judgment; many of the people staffing these offices are former newspaper, magazine, radio, and television reporters and have a keen sense for what makes news.

Working with a media relations specialist should be a partnership. You share a responsibility to develop a narrative based on your work or expertise that would be of news interest. Their job and yours is to determine what your story is and why people should care.

These in-house media professionals should be skilled at identifying and developing stories of news interest from your institution and presenting this information to the press. They have a good sense of the media and their story needs. Their success comes from establishing professional relationships with the press. The best media relations professionals know the story interests of the reporters they are contacting and guard against taking up their time with information about programs and events that are not news. Those in the media keep lists, mentally and physically, of media relations people who waste their time trying to pitch non-stories. Those who do quickly lose their professional standing with members of the press who no longer see them as resources but instead as people to ignore.

If the media relations staff does not think you have a story, ask why and what it would take to make one. It might mean connecting your work to an upcoming news event such as an important anniversary date, or congressional hearings on a topic related to your story, or linking it to a trend that might involve including the work of other scholars, which could add value to the story.

Do not try to force your work on media relations when the staff does not agree on its news importance, which I find happens often. I frequently find a certain level of frustration among some faculty and administrators with the staff at the media relations office when I visit a college or university. It seems to stem from a mutual lack of communication between media relations and its campus constituents. For starters, there may be a general misunderstanding on the role of the media relations office and the reality of its business. It does not control the news. From presidents to administrators to faculty, I have heard more than once how they want the media relations office to place a story for them on the front page of the *New York Times*, and as one vice president of development requested, above the fold. Media coverage is not advertising. You cannot order it up. It must be earned.

Another area of mutual frustration is the seemingly all-too-often response that it's not news when staff in media relations is asked to promote a program or event. Odds are the media relations staff is right. Staff members may wish it were news; however, they know the media will turn it down and wonder why the media relations office doesn't know better.

Don't walk away when media relations staff tells you that what you are presenting is not news. See it as a starting point to work with staff members and to develop a long-term media strategy. Form a partnership with media relations to identify areas of your work that could be of news interest. Keep the staff abreast of upcoming developments in your field. Study what has generated coverage in the past and suggest areas of future news interest. Remember, generating positive news coverage is a process, and there are a number of steps you can take can increase your odds for success.

Working With a Media Consultant

Sometimes the best option to generate media coverage may be to work with a media consultant. Consulting firms around the country specialize in providing media services for nonprofit institutions. The best media relations firms for scholars and researchers have a strong working knowledge of the academy and the scientific community. They know the language, the issues, and the culture of the professions. They have a track record of success in presenting stories to the media and generating meaningful coverage for their clients.

You might consider working with a media consultant when the in-house public relations staff feels the demands of your project are greater than it has time to provide. This might be for a major research announcement or a long-term effort to advance social or policy change. Work with your public relations office to determine the option best for you. Look to its staff for recommendations of names of consultants to interview, and include staff members in the process of deciding which is the best firm to hire. Should you hire a media consultant, keep the campus media relations office in the loop with regard to the consultant's media plan and activities, such as providing the names of the media the consultant will be contacting on your behalf.

The following are factors to consider in hiring a media consultant:

1. Working with a consultant is going to take more of your time, not less. It is a partnership that will require your strong and ongoing participation. The consultant will be asking you to take an active role in media strategy and story development. Chances are you will be asked to write opinion articles and letters to the editor, meet with the media, and respond to media calls. Media relations will need to become a priority on your schedule.

2. Do not hire on price alone. The most expensive consultant does not necessarily mean that you will receive the best service or results. The least expensive, on the other hand, can become quite costly when you see little or no return from your money spent.

3. Do not pay for the address. Even though a firm's office may be located on Madison Avenue, an expense you will be paying for, it does not mean that its consultants have any stronger connections with journalists than the media relations specialists from Poughkeepsie or elsewhere. It is not the address that media professionals care about, it is the story.

4. See where you fit in among the consultant's clients. You do not want to be a little fish in a big pond. If you are, odds are the junior executive will be handling your account. And just because the firm has had success in promoting commercial accounts does not mean its expertise, style, and media contacts will successfully transfer to serving nonprofits.

5. Hire the person you will be working with, not the person selling the account. One may be impressive while the other is not. Remember, it is a partnership that you will be establishing with the account representative, and his or her skills, personality, and professionalism matter.

6. Ask to talk with current and past clients. Were they satisfied with the services? What were the results? How much of their time was required? Were there any problems? If they are no longer working with the consultant, why? Was it an overall positive experience and worth the investment?

7. The services a consultant offers should not be an all-or-nothing proposition. Many media consultants' proposals I have read seem to go overboard with their institutional audits, media training, story development, press kits, special events, and press conferences they propose to the client. These all are important components in the media relations process, but determining which ones are best for you and the degree to which they are provided should be a conversation between you and the consultant. Be realistic. What are the odds, for example, of your appearing on national television, and do you really need two days of media training sitting in front of a consultant's camera? Could. Maybe. Might. But often not. However, if you are one of those few who have a good shot at appearing on the *Today* show, go for it.

8. Focus on the basics. Don't let an elaborate proposal obscure the reasons you are hiring a consultant. What matters is feeling confident that the firm you hire understands your story

and believes it has meaningful news value, and that it will be in direct contact with important and targeted media outlets. This information should be clearly and prominently presented in the media plan.

Price, time, fit, and a history of success all matter when hiring a media consultant. But the bottom line is, you want to know this: How does the consultant define your story? And how and to whom will he or she tell it?

CHAPTER NINE

Presenting New
Research Findings

Media want to report on major new research findings that relate to the interests of their readers and viewers. Discovering a new planet, identifying a new ocean species, deciphering an ancient text, or developing a new vaccine for a major disease are sure bets for media coverage. Reporters in popular media, such as daily newspapers, weekly news magazines, and network news, regularly scan scholarly journals like *Science, Nature, Cell, American Journal of Sociology, American Anthropologist,* and many more, in search of new story ideas.

Journal editors know this, and some send advance copies of upcoming issues to the mainstream media for an early look. Information usually is embargoed until the official journal release date. However, receiving early copies allows reporters to plan ahead and gives them added time to investigate and understand the significance of the findings.

Not all reporters appreciate receiving embargoed news releases. Some feel it is a manipulation of the news and do not want to be part of an orchestrated event. Others put up with it, says one national science reporter who writes for a major weekly news magazine but resists any attempts to be spoon-fed the news. The other response, which I hear much more often when it comes to the release of major reports, is that they appreciate receiving advance copies, which gives them the opportunity to do their best reporting on often complicated subjects.

Journalists in popular media value the peer review process, although they know it is not without fault, and they look to the professional journals to take the lead in identifying and validating important new research. From time to time the press has been stung by reporting scientific announcements that bypassed peer review. This is sometimes referred to as "science by press conference."

One of the first reports of this was made in a March 27, 1980, *New England Journal of Medicine* commentary: "In recent months, however, we have begun to witness a reversal unheard of in the annals of scientific communication: the phenomenon of scientists publishing research data by press conference." The author, Spyros Andreopoulos, a member of the Stanford University Medical Center News Bureau, expressed concern over reporting the latest developments in the field of recombinant DNA research. "The method of disclosure," he wrote, "was not through the accepted channels of scientific communication, but by press conference in which unpublished data were presented by scientists and accepted by the press as valid." He said a press announcement in September 1978 by Genentech, "a small research company in San Francisco," released news about a new discovery instead of presenting it first in a refereed journal. Andreopoulos said that "journalists reported it as a 'breakthrough,' failing to ask critical questions that would have helped place the work in perspective."(1)

Media organizations have since reported on archeologists' finding of an ancient lost city in the rain forests of Peru and a chemist's creation of cold fusion in a bottle, only to find later that neither discovery as presented was true. The stories of these misreported events then became the headlines, generating significant amounts of unfavorable media coverage for the researchers and their institutions.

Shortly after a major announcement of a sighting of an ivory-billed woodpecker, once believed to be extinct, in the swampy forests of Arkansas, an international debate quickly surfaced within the ornithology community challenging the finding, which gained wide media attention. "The rush to release the discovery of the ivory-billed woodpecker was wrong," said a professor of biological sciences who has been closely following the events after the announcement. "They should have waited until the facts were in." "There is a better chance of filming Sasquatch than the ivory-billed woodpecker," he said with a smile.

Don't jump the gun in releasing new research findings. Goals to increase fund-raising, prestige, and getting there first, which one scientist believes drives many early research announcements, can quickly be washed overboard when the media discovers that your news fails to withstand the rigor of review.

However, media professionals are of two minds when it comes to relying on science journals for their news. Holcomb Noble, a former *New York Times* deputy director of science news, said in a 1986 interview during the heyday of science reporting by the popular press,

> [W]e don't like to rely exclusively on those or any other journal, especially in medicine. If a new drug is reported on and doctors are talking about it, we don't feel we have to wait until it appears in a peer-reviewed journal. Not when there's something out there in the

field that has the potential for saving lives, but nobody knows about it because it's backed up on the queue waiting to be published in the medical journal. That's bad for patients, for people, and it's bad for the flow of information.(2)

Professional and Trade Journals

Professional and trade journals, such as *Chemical Week*, *Chronicle of Higher Education*, and *Harvard Business Review,* are quick to spot new developments in their areas of coverage and often reach a broader audience than a peer-reviewed journal might. *IEEE Spectrum*, the publication for electrical and electronics engineers, does an excellent job of reaching a professional and a lay audience interested in following new scientific and technical developments.

It is not often apparent in the presentation of new research why the public would be interested. Professional and trade journals can be the stepping-stone from a refereed journal, which only a specialist in the field might appreciate reading, to the mainstream media. Coverage in professional and trade journals is valuable for its own sake, but consider them too as a way to present your research to a broader range of media.

Reporters for these journals do not shy away from complicated subjects and dense reports when searching for interesting new developments in the field they cover. They have the knowledge to translate the more technical material and make it interesting to professional and educated lay audiences who read their publication. A professional or trade journal article can bring greater clarity to new research, which may not have been apparent to the mainstream media. They also serve to further validate the accuracy and importance of the research.

When I approach popular media outlets such as *Business Week* or *Time* about new research findings, one of the strongest selling points I have is to let them know that this new work will be appearing in an upcoming issue of a peer-reviewed, professional, or trade journal. It is the Good Housekeeping Seal of Approval they often look for and value. Those in the mainstream media generally see professional and trade publications as supports to their work and not as competition. These insiders' publications are early spotters of news and trends for the media and the public.

Science Reporting by the Mainstream Media

We tend to mostly remember when the press gets it wrong, but the reality is that major national press organizations are great at reporting on new research, taking complicated theories and practices and making them interesting to the public. It's quite a feat when you take into account the tight story deadlines these writers routinely face, and that they are able to explain sophisticated research with a high degree of intelligence and accuracy, making it interesting to people of all generations and varying levels of education, from the grade school student to the PhD.

In fact, one newspaper editor was so good at understanding the sciences that he even corrected Albert Einstein. It is a wonderful story, as reported by "R. D." in a 1984 article in *The Quill*:

Carr Van Anda, managing editor of *The New York Times* from 1904 to 1932, was a mathematician with serious interest in astronomy and physics, and was largely responsible for bringing Einstein's revolutionary work to the attention of the American public. When Einstein came to lecture at Princeton in the early 1920s, the

Times reported the event from translations prepared at the university. Meyer Berger in his *The Story of The New Times*, recounts Dean Christian Gauss's recollection of what happened when a translation reached Van Anda:

"It came at a time . . . when relativity was only understood by Dr. Einstein and by the Deity. When we sent up the translation, Dr. Einstein had already lost even the professorial mathematicians who were here to hear him, but the *Times* called me before going to press to ask whether there was not some mistake in the figures.

"I called up Professor Adams. He had translated the lectures for us and had made abstracts for the newspapers. I told him that Mr. Van Anda thought one of the equations was wrong. Adams searched his notes and said, 'No, that is what Einstein said.'

"I told Mr. Adams that I took Mr. Van Anda very seriously, so he worked a while longer on his notes. Finally he called me back. He said, 'I am going to call Dr. Einstein.' When Einstein was consulted he was astonished. He scanned the notes and nodded. He said, 'Yes, Mr. Van Anda is right. I made a mistake in transcribing the equation on the blackboard.'"(3)

The zenith of popular science reporting was in the late 1970s and early 1980s. The *New York Times* led the parade of science reporting with the introduction of its highly regarded Science Times section in 1978, the country's oldest newspaper science section. Newspapers nationwide followed suit, and by 1986 the number of weekly science sections appearing in daily newspapers totaled 66.(4) These sections, as they do now, covered science, technology, health, medicine, and other related topics.

Dedicated popular science magazines were quick to follow. Publications geared to the lay audience included *Discover*, *Omni*, *Next*, *Science 80* (its name changing to reflect the current year until its demise in 1986). The weekly news magazines, *Time*, *Newsweek*, *U.S. News & World Report*, each developed strong science reporting. Television was the next in line, introducing such science series as PBS's *Cosmos*, *Odyssey*, and *Nova*, and CBS's *Universe*.

Today, the *New York Times* Science Times still reigns as the newspaper leader in science, medical, health, and technology reporting. Other newspapers and major broadcast networks have cut back in science reporting because of tightened budgets and shrinking news space.

However, the overall quality of science, medical, health, and technology reporting seems to have steadily grown over these past three decades. More reporters covering these fields for the popular press come with academic backgrounds in science, technology, engineering, and mathematics. NBC chief science and health correspondent Robert Bazell earned a doctoral candidate degree in immunology from the University of California at Berkley.(5) Daniel Wilson, host of the History Channel's *The Works*, has a PhD in robotics.(6)

As a sign of the times, *U.S. News & World Report* editor Brian Kelly wrote in an editor's note that "science subjects are becoming sexier." The challenge for the reporters, he said, is that "science is one of those subjects that can move a little slowly for some of us in the news business. It's hard to craft a taut narrative around a couple decades' worth of research in the lab. Or a million years of evolution. Then one day, whatever's been brewing changes the world."(7)

A National Research Council study titled "Public Participation in Environmental Assessment and Decision Making" found that when correctly implemented public participation improves the quality of decisions about the environment. "Public participation can help get the science right and get the right science," said the head of the panel overseeing the study. It is "the melding together of science and democracy."(8)

Working with media to accurately report new science findings and policy is an essential component when attempting to successfully inform, educate, and seek public participation in developing an understanding of science and good decision making.

What Makes a Good Research Story

The British magazine *New Scientist* provides a good overview of what it considers to be news, which can be applied in varying degrees to other science (and nonscientific) publications as well, in the following guidelines for submissions:

> We will never run a feature on new research just because it is worthy or important. There has to be something extra about it too. The kinds of features we are looking for generally fit into one of the following categories:
>
> Ideas or discoveries that overturn important ideas in science.
>
> Ideas, discoveries or inventions that overturn common assumptions.
>
> Ideas or discoveries that just make you go WOW!
>
> Discoveries that answer long-standing questions in science.
>
> New technologies that could change the way the world works.
>
> Fun, quirky or unusual stories with a science angle.
>
> The definitive guide to . . . (e.g., climate myths).
>
> The kinds of features we aren't looking for:
>
> An important step forward in an area of science that non-specialists neither know nor care about (e.g., "New fossil forces radical rethink in mudstone geology").
>
> A discovery that moves an important area of science forward very slightly (e.g., cancer vaccine shown to work in rare form of carcinoma).
>
> A progress report on some area of science that has been ticking along nicely but uneventfully for years.
>
> An extraordinary idea that isn't backed by a genuine researcher and/or a peer reviewed paper.
>
> Stories that are about projects or techniques rather than results.
>
> Stories about people rather than science.
>
> Stories that have local rather than global significance.
>
> Any idea where the science is shoehorned in where it doesn't belong (e.g., The immune challenges to being born in a stable/

The science of the Olympics/The science of any sci-fi TV show or film).(9)

Planting the Story Seed

If you have a journal article scheduled to appear that you believe has the potential for mainstream media interest, talking and meeting with key reporters ahead of the publication date to discuss its importance on an embargoed basis can be an effective way to generate accurate and meaningful coverage at the time of its official release. First you will want the OK from the journal's editor to share embargoed copies of the article; in this way you can open up opportunities for your story to be more widely reported.

You can assume that the best reporters covering your field are inundated with advance material about upcoming reports. In their world, there is no shortage of good stories to choose from. Your material can be sent in advance, but it probably will join a stack of other pending reports looking for attention. Making a phone call, noting why you believe your study would be of interest to the reporter's audience, following up with e-mail, and possibly setting up an appointment to meet create opportunities to be heard. Your goal is to see meaningful coverage in the mainstream media stemming from the journal article on the day or shortly after it is released. You are not trying to supersede the journal's publication date but coincide with it. Letting media know about your new research a few days or a week after the journal article appears risks its being seen as old news. Your best opportunities for coverage may have passed. Sure, if it is a revolutionary new development, little or no advance work is required. The news will capture media's attention and you can enjoy the ride. However, most research doesn't have that immediate wow factor. It needs an added push for mainstream media to appreciate its public importance and for it to be seen as news.

Philosopher Ralph Waldo Emerson's observation about capturing his own attention can be applied to media as well: "What attracts my attention shall have it, as I will go to the man who knocks on my door, whilst a thousand persons, as worthy, go by it, to whom I give no regard."(10)

Select a reporter or news outlet you believe can best tell your story. Make contact by phone or e-mail to introduce yourself and your story. Tell the reporter you would like to discuss your research more fully. If the person is interested, ask if he or she agrees to the terms of the embargo. If so, you and the reporter have an opportunity to fully discuss the nature and importance of your work about to be released. It allows the reporter a deeper understanding of the findings and their significance and gives the reporter an opportunity to prepare and do his or her best job.

It is critical to remember that you are not agreeing to let the reporter break the news earlier than anyone else, even by an hour. He or she is held to the same time restrictions set for the embargo as the other media.

Other reporters might argue that this is playing favorites, and it is in one sense. But it does not prohibit them from picking up the phone and talking with you when they receive an early copy of the release, and it does not put them behind any other reporters in the official release of the story. Reporting the news cuts both ways: It can be generated through the media's initiative or through yours.

The truth is, not all media organizations are equal, and some outlets are better suited at reaching the audiences that are more important to you than others. And not all reporters are equal; some are more skilled to write about your research than others. The key to releasing complicated scientific and technical data is seeing that it is accurately reported. Your advance work can help ensure this. The reporter scholars contact is often the one who has been showing an interest in their work and has earned their early attention.

Embargoes

Some professionals in the media hate them, they can be confusing and sometimes broken, but embargoes attempt to put order in events and allow time for more thorough reporting about complex issues and findings. The National Association of Science Writers' Web site states that "many newspaper reporters prepare their stories well in advance of their deadlines. This applies especially to science stories, which often take considerable time to write. This lead time is the primary reason advance texts are so important."(11)

Because a media outlet receives an embargoed release does not mean it will choose to honor it. I've seen a number of them broken (see, for example, p. 41 in chapter 4). That is the risk you take; however, the large majority of media professionals honor embargoes. But remember, as soon as one news outlet releases the story, the embargo is considered off, and it becomes fair game for all media to report.

Releases often carry an embargo with a date and time: "Embargoed. Not for release until: 10:00 a.m. (EST), September 4, 2010." The date and time usually coincides with a press event, such as a conference to officially announce the news in the release. Before the Internet and its 24-hour news cycle, a morning embargo time allowed the afternoon newspapers and evening television newscasts to report the news. An afternoon release time favored the morning newspapers. Radio was in between, often reporting what was in the newspapers. Embargoes worked for some of the media but not for others who felt they lost a day in reporting the news because the time restriction worked against them.

Today, news that is embargoed can appear on the Web at the exact moment it is released. The Web has leveled the playing field in the reporting of information, and all media outlets have an opportunity to post the story on their news sites at the same time, whether the site is a morning newspaper or an evening television newscast.

However, the least cumbersome embargoes for you and the media are those without a time of day restriction: "Embargoed. For release November 19, 2010." This allows the majority of the media to run the story the day of the release with less chance of the embargo's being broken because of confusion over time zone differences.

Press Conferences

This can be a misnomer. Conferences that are billed for the press often have few media representatives attending. Too many press conferences I've seen are more for show than a place where important news is being announced. When the story is missing, these kinds of publicity events waste money and time, and do little or nothing to advance meaningful media coverage.

Organizers of these failed events mistakenly think that calling them press conferences will bring the media. They often don't. When no major news will be announced, the important media organizations stay away. They don't have the time to sit through an event and not walk away with a story.

Colleges, universities, foundations, institutes, businesses—you name it—seem to love Washington, D.C., as the setting to hold a press conference. Organizers seem to think the importance of place will carry their story. When I've attended these press conferences, I find the room can be filled but not with the media. The guests may represent other important audiences such as fellow scholars, legislative aides, policy group staffers, and the host's board members, but the big media organizations (the reason that all the money was spent to put on the show) are often not present. Maybe there will be a few reporters, possibly representing a trade magazine or newsletter, a small wire service, or a publication I didn't know existed, but I've rarely seen a meaningful presence of the major media. If you truly have a major announcement that is important to the media in the town where you hold the event, have a press conference to release the news. Short of that, save your money and don't waste the media's time.

Notes

1. Andreopoulos, S. (1980, March 27). Gene Cloning by Press Conference. *New England Journal of Medicine, 302*, 743–746.

2. Science Section Staffers Speak. (1986, Autumn). *SIPIscope, 14*(4), p. 16.

3. R. D. (1984, June). Scientific Editing. *The Quill*, p. 27.

4. U.S. Dailies with Weekly Science Sections. (1986, Autumn). *SIPIscope, 14*(4), p. 12.

5. *Robert Bazell Chief Science and Health Correspondent*. (2008, October 29). Retrieved March 5, 2009, from http://www.msnbc.msn.com/id/3687100/

6. Keveney, B. (2008, July 21). Catch the Beach TV Wave This Summer. Retrieved January 2, 2010, from *USA Today*: http://www.usatoday.com/life/television/news/2008-07-17-beach-TV_N.htm

7. Kelly, B. (2008, August 4–11). Tackling the Big Questions. *U.S. News & World Report*, p. 5.

8. Dean, C. (2008, August 23). Report Says Public Outreach, Done Right, Aids Policymaking. Retrieved January 2, 2010, from the *New York Times*: http://www.nytimes.com/2008/08/23/science/wacad.html?_r=1&

scp = 1&sq = report%20says%20public%20outreach%20done%20right&
st = cse

9. New Scientist Feature Guidelines. (2008, April). Personal communication.

10. Emerson, R. *Essays: First Series: Spiritual Laws (1841)*. Retrieved November 27, 2009, from Emerson Central: http://www.emersoncentral.com/spirituallaws.htm

11. National Association of Science Writers. (2006, August 28). *Release Dates and Times*. Retrieved January 2, 2010, from http://www.nasw.org/resource/pios/csn/reldate.htm

CHAPTER TEN

When a Reporter Calls

I think reporters are often surprised at how much information people, particularly those without media experience, freely reveal to them in interviews just because they asked. The person being interviewed relinquishes control of the discussion and lets the reporter take over. It is as though he or she is a witness at a court hearing, dutifully answering all the judge's questions.

It's good to be helpful, but you need to establish checks and balances in every media discussion. For starters, when someone from the media calls, verify whom you are speaking to. What is the person's name? Ask the person to spell it. What media outlet does he or she represent? What is the person's title, telephone number, and e-mail address? Why is he or she calling? Is it for a story? If the person is a freelance writer, ask if the story has been commissioned by a particular media outlet, or if he or she is writing it on spec (speculation, hoping to sell it later). If you are unfamiliar with the news outlet the reporter represents, ask for more information. If you are still uncertain, ask the person to send you some background information, including the organization's Web address. Say you will call back after you have had a chance to review the information. This verification process should not be a problem for legitimate media professionals, and it should only be a matter of minutes for them to send you something electronically.

The answers to these questions can determine how much time, if any, you want to invest in the interview. If you need a little time to collect your thoughts, tell the reporter you would be glad to speak with him or her, but now is not a good time to talk. Schedule an appointment for a discussion, whether it's in 10 minutes or for the next day. Putting it off too long, however, risks losing the interview.

Should you wish to continue the discussion, ask the reporter who else will be interviewed for the article if that is important to you. Knowing this can give you insight into the direction the article may take and can shape your responses. Ask when the article is expected to appear. Will you have a chance to review your quotes prior to publication? Some reporters do not have a problem with this, others do. You need to know what your response will be if the answer is no. If the answer is yes, this does not give you license to edit the entire article; you may only verify the accuracy of your quotes.

Your intent in asking these questions isn't to scare the reporter away or to needlessly take up his or her time but to have a clear understanding of what you are being asked to comment on and with whom you are speaking. Set some ground rules that work for both of you. Keep in mind the five *F*s in establishing a good working relationship with the media: deal with them in a manner that is fast, factual, frank, fair, and friendly.(1) Another tip is to stand up when taking a challenging phone call from a reporter. Standing can help you focus your thoughts and distance you from the distractions on your desk.

Spare Me

When talking with a reporter, don't speak Klingon, even if you are both attending a Star Trek convention. *National Journal* columnist William Powers said in an *American Journalism Review* article that "most academics are used to giving long, tortured answers to a question that work in the academic world but don't work for a quotation. A lot of experts get called but never get used because they're boring and dull."(2)

"Stories that use academic experts are often stories built around ideas," a newspaper editor told me. "For a reporter, it's important that the source engage on the idea, not talk about other things. If you don't want to do that for whatever reason, say so."

Marshall Wittmann, a senior fellow at the Democratic Leadership Council, said that "skilled commentators know intuitively what a reporter is looking for and can give it to them a few minutes into the interview. Reporters want someone who will say something interesting. Reporters don't want something wonky. They want something that encapsulates the point they are trying to make."(3)

Look at the difference in the following responses to a reporter's question during an interview: "It is often useful, for purposes of understanding a contemporaneous happening, to engage in counterfactual historical speculation," one professor said.

Another simply answered, "Just imagine."(4)

Notes

1. Cutlip, S., & Center, A. (1978). *Effective Public Relations* (5th ed.), p. 389. Englewood Cliffs, NJ: Prentice-Hall.

2. Cohen, M. (2005, April/May). The Quote Machines. *American Journalism Review.* Retrieved November 21, 2008, from http://www.ajr.org/article_printable.asp?id = 3857

3. Cohen, The Quote Machines.

4. Quinn, K. (1992, April/May). Courting the Great Gray Lady. *Lingua Franca,* pp. 27–29.

CHAPTER ELEVEN

The Media Interview

Nothing in the media's processes seems to create more fear in people than the interview. People's concerns usually center on "What might I say wrong?" and "Will I be misquoted?" Each is a legitimate issue, but good preparation can make this experience, which may seem akin to a trip to the dentist, productive and satisfying. Many faculty I work with often look forward to being interviewed.

Certainly there are times when a media interview can be tense and adversarial, such as when responding to a crisis or allegations of misdeeds. During these times, even major media personalities such as celebrities and television news anchors who might be the unwelcome focus of the news will avoid being interviewed by reporters. I assume they fear that the risk of making a situation worse for themselves is too great. For instance, the chairman and publisher of the *New York Times*, Arthur Sulzberger Jr., and other company executives declined to be interviewed by a *Times* reporter about the fiscal health of the newspaper; the subject was seemingly too sensitive for them to be quoted on, even by their own paper.(1)

However, interviews that are built around presenting new story ideas or adding insight into important news and developments can be rewarding. Faculty seem to be particularly adroit with interviews because they focus on teaching and learning for the reporter and the scholar. The reporter is learning what is on the scholar's mind and the scholar is gaining insight into the needs of the story, offering new information to enhance the reporter's knowledge of the topic. For faculty who enjoy teaching, it is another opportunity to help someone learn and to better inform the public about important matters.

Comparing the media interview to the teaching and learning experience, James Zull, a professor of biology at Case Western Reserve University, offers excellent advice in *The Art of Changing the Brain*. Listing some of the ways people learn, Zull said that for teachers to connect with their students, or in our case with reporters, they should "Repeat, repeat, repeat!" key messages, "Construct metaphors," and "Use analogies and similes," to effectively drive home important points, or as he says, "change brains."(2) These teaching skills readily transfer to media interviews and can effectively convey your story.

A good example is an NPR interview with former U.S. Secretary of the Treasury and Harvard University professor Lawrence Summers regarding the collapse of the American housing market and the state of the national economy. Summers helped listeners understand the sometimes complicated forces driving these economic events through his skillful use of metaphors, similes, and repetition of key points.

The following are excerpts from his on-air discussion with Tom Ashbrook, host of NPR's *On Point*:

Tom Ashbrook (*TA*): Are we in economic crisis?
Lawrence Summers (*LS*): Fever has perhaps broken slightly in [the] last several weeks.

If you look at financial crises they're all the same. Greed and
   leverage.
Lending levels take off, but trees don't grow to the sky.
Like [the] 13th chime of a clock, it causes people to doubt all that
   came before.
TA (asking about the changed Federal Reserve Bank role): Will they
   be more interventionist than they've ever been?
LA: Certainly [it] will be hard to put the genie completely back in
   the bottle.
TA: Is it the wrong medicine then?
LA: If you have a fire, you have to sort of decide what kind of fire
   it is. If it's a grease fire, spraying water on it is going to make it
   worse. Is it a more conventional fire, in which case water is the
   answer? What types of approaches are right to the fire? You sort
   of have to decide those issues before you decide how the fire
   department is going to be organized.
TA (asking about the federal bailout for at-risk mortgage holders):
LS: The fact that somebody smoked in bed is not usually thought
   of as a reason not to call the fire department, particularly when
   their house is very near other houses.(3)

Science and business writer Ben Daviss, who has interviewed a
number of scholars and researchers for his articles in major
national and international publications, believes that a goal in giving an interview should be to "make interesting ideas and developments accessible" to readers and viewers. "This doesn't require
dumbing down the language," he says. "It is about being clear and
concise." He recommends that scholars offering interviews take
time to explain their work, be patient, take it slowly; use analogies
of everyday things to relate complicated ideas; and develop an elevator summary of their work, they can go back to elaborate. He
said that giving a detailed explanation is not generally helpful to
reporters. "When I ask what time it is, I don't want to hear how a
watch is made." An editor for a major newspaper said, "How

much detail provided varies with reporters and media outlets: a *New York Times* specialist may want a lot, a general assignment reporter less and simpler."

The following are important guidelines in preparing for and taking part in a media interview, both for print and broadcast.

Media Interview Checklist

1. Be yourself. It establishes credibility.
2. Be prepared. Anticipate questions and develop answers that clearly state the key ideas you want to express. Limit your list of key points to two or three.
3. Be enthusiastic. It comes across as conviction.
4. Be specific. Use short answers and avoid jargon. Use clear and simple language. State the most important facts first. Keep your response focused on the question. Don't volunteer more information than needed.
5. Be correct. Don't guess at answers. It's OK to say "I don't know" and "I'll get back to you with the information."
6. Be anecdotal. Anecdotes help fix a point in the listener's mind.
7. Be a listener. How well you listen to questions is as important as how well you respond.
8. Be cool. Hostile questions do not demand hostile answers.
9. Be truthful. Never lie. Your credibility depends on it.
10. Don't let the reporter put words in your mouth. Some reporters might say, "So in other words you're saying . . ." Correct inaccuracies. Don't allow the reporter's errors to slip by. Keep your corrections to the point. If the reporter's question contains offensive language, do not repeat it.

11. Formulate your response for the public. The public, not the media, is your real audience.

12. Repeat important points you wish to make throughout the interview. Summarize these points at the end of the discussion.

13. Ask the reporter questions. You can often tell from his or her answers whether your remarks have been understood.

14. Don't say anything you would not want to see in print or heard on the air. Saying something off the record is no guarantee that it will be. The interview is never over until you and the reporter have parted company.(4)

Remember too that when you are in front of or near a studio camera or microphone, you must present yourself at all times as though you are being recorded. Too many professionals, from major politicians and public figures to seasoned network newscasters, have embarrassed themselves on air when they mistakenly believed the cameras or microphones were turned off.

The Reverend Jesse Jackson suffered public fallout for his "hurtful and wrong" comments he made about Senator Barack Obama when he mistakenly thought his microphone was turned off during a break from taping a Fox News interview. "For any harm or hurt that this hot mic private conversation may have caused, I apologize."(5) For days Jackson's unintended public statements dominated the news.

When President George W. Bush thought he was not being recorded during a public appearance, a subsequent newspaper headline read, "Bush tells crowd at GOP fundraiser 'Wall Street got drunk.'" According to *USA Today*, "President Bush asked everyone to turn off their video cameras before he commented on the economy at a GOP fundraiser last week in Houston. . . . At least one person ignored his request. Footage of the president's appearance is now available online."(6)

Terms of Engagement

The news business has its own terminology for conducting interviews, and it is important to understand it before talking with a reporter. Unless you tell a reporter differently *before the interview and he or she agrees to your terms,* all information you discuss is considered *on the record.* The following are some common terms:

On the record means that what you say is for quotation and attribution. All that you say can be reported, and you will be identified as the source of the information.

Background means that what you said can be reported but not attributed. Or as *New York Times* "On Language" columnist William Safire wrote, "Background is for direct quotation with the source muddied, such as 'a source close to the investigation.'"(7)

Off the record means the information provided is not for publication. "Material that is really *off the record* cannot be used in the story, period," states a leading text for training journalists.(8) However, the authors said, off the record is a term that can mean different things to different reporters, let alone to their editors. In an *American Journalism Review* article about the confusion within journalism over the meaning of this and other interview terms, Edward Pound, a reporter for *U.S. News & World Report*, offered his interpretation: "It means I can't use it unless I can get it elsewhere. . . . Most sources don't understand it. They tend to think off the record and on background mean the same thing."(9) Avoid going off the record in an interview. Media professionals often don't like it, and there are no guarantees your words won't come back to bite you.

Samantha Powers, a Pulitzer Prize–winning author and noted war journalist, resigned her position as senior foreign policy adviser to presidential candidate Barack Obama because of a remark she made to a Scottish newspaper about Hillary Rodham Clinton; she called Clinton a "monster." These remarks were supposed to have been off the record, Powers said, but the newspaper printed them. In a later interview with the *New York Times* she said her "careless words (about Senator Clinton) had eclipsed, at least for now, her life's work."(10)

Keep matters simple and your interview on the record. If there is something that you do not want reported, don't say it. In the hundreds of interviews of college and university presidents, faculty, researchers, and the media that I have participated in over the years, there was rarely a case that information discussed was presented off the record.

Rabbit Stew

What tips do reporters receive in their training about conducting an interview and getting the story? In the classic journalism textbook, *New Survey of Journalism*, author George Fox Mott advised would-be and new reporters, "Before you can have rabbit stew, first catch the rabbit." To set snares to catch the interviewee off guard and possibly reveal more than he or she might care to, Mott offered hints that have "the endorsement of many well-known interviewers." Here are a few:

> Keep the atmosphere of the interview as informal as possible. Avoid unnecessary mention of the word "interview."
>
> The indirect approach to the subject is often the best. Get a man to talk about his hobbies or other subjects in which he is especially interested and which can be related to the main topic on which you are interviewing him.

Unless the interviewee wishes to be quoted verbatim, avoid the use of a notebook or the too-apparent note-taking since this often makes him aware that he is going to be quoted and causes him to speak less freely. If note-taking is necessary, do it unobtrusively. Better still, listen attentively and as soon as the interview is over make notes on the essential information.(11)

Do not be the rabbit in the stew. Stay focused and on point.

A reporter once asked me about my hobbies during an interview about my work with the national media. Bingo! I told him all about my interest in restoring vintage cars and took him to my home to show off my projects. Can you smell the rabbit stew cooking? It was classic. He had gotten me in a comfort zone and my guard was down. Readers learned from the newspaper article about my work with the media but also about all those old cars that "did not start." It was harmless, but it was a reminder of a reporter's skills in getting a story.

Reporters have a stock of standard questions that can apply to just about all topics, and often they ask them at the beginning of interviews. The ones I hear when reporters sit down to talk with faculty include such conversation starters as, Tell me about your work. Why is it important? Why is it different? What's new? Why should people care? What are the key issues? What is most surprising? What keeps you up at night? What are your biggest concerns? What do you want to see happen next? CNN legendary talk show host Larry King's stock-in-trade question, regardless of the guest or the issue, is, "Whaddaya make of it?"

As simple as these questions may first appear, some people are taken aback when asked to respond. They may have come into interviews armed with facts and figures about their work but become tongue-tied when asked such open-ended questions. A lot of "uhs" and "ahs" fill the air. Some may remember the famous

televised interview between CBS newsman Roger Mudd and Senator Ted Kennedy regarding his 1980 run for president. The question that caught Kennedy off guard was, "Senator, why do you
want to be president?" Kennedy, as he stumbled over his words
searching for an answer, responded: "Well, I'm—were I to make
the announcement to run, the reasons that I would run is because
I have a great belief in this country that it is—has more natural
resources than any nation of the world."(12)

The tough questions asked by reporters are often saved until
last. In the journalism textbook *Writing & Reporting the News*,
authors Gerald Lanson and Mitchell Stephens advise would-be
journalists to save their tough questions for the end. "By the end
of the interview you have less to lose by alienating subjects, and
after a long interview they might be more inclined to let down
their guard." One newspaper reporter Lanson and Stephens quote
reveals that "he sometimes get[s] his best material 'after' the formal interview is over and his pad and pen have been tucked
away."(13)

Fiction and truth seem to merge in the novel *Airframe*, as author
Michael Crichton gives readers a hard look, as he sees it, at the
world of modern journalism and the challenges that lie waiting
when interviewed by a reporter:

Walking away from him, she realized she was exhausted by the
efforts of the interview. Talking to a reporter these days was like a
deadly chess match; you had to think several steps ahead; you had
to imagine all the possible ways a reporter might distort your statement.
    Because the focus was so personal, the reporters asked continu-
ously for personal speculations. Do you think an event will be dam-
aging? Do you think the company will suffer? Such speculation had
been irrelevant to the earlier generation of reporters, who focused

on the underlying events. Modern journalism was intensely subjective—"interpretive"—and speculation was its lifeblood. But she
found it exhausting.

And Jack Rogers, she thought, was one of the better ones. The
print reporters were all better. It was the television reporters you
really had to watch out for. They were the really dangerous ones.
(14)

Another modern author, Tom Wolfe, talked about reporters'
singular mission in an interview. "There is an attitude [with
reporters]," he said. "And that attitude is: 'You have some information. I desperately need that information—and I deserve it!'
That's the attitude. It gives you the willpower to go up to strangers
and ask questions and demand answers you have no right to
know."(15)

These are all points to consider as you prepare for an interview,
but don't be led off course from making the interview your opportunity to tell your story. Keep focused, stay calm, and present your
key points clearly and concisely. Thinking ahead to the next question and avoiding speculative comments, ambiguous language,
and phrases that easily could be taken out of context are essential
lessons to be learned and practiced in giving a successful interview.

Avoiding Media Blunders

When someone is quoted and he or she does not like how the
quote appeared in print, it is often because the comment was made
offhand during the interview. The person might have thought it
was obvious to the reporter that he or she was making an exaggerated remark or a joke and never considered it would end up in
print, for example, "I thought he was crazy," or "That was the
dumbest thing I've ever heard." In another scenario, after a formal

interview at a newspaper or television station, the reporter walks his or her guest to the exit, both engaged in a friendly chat before parting company. During these unguarded moments the reporter may uncover his or her best quotes, catching the interviewee in a relaxed mood and eliciting a comment or two taken out of context. All is on the record unless otherwise agreed upon, and this unfettered language may be added to the reporter's story.

When to Ask for a Correction

Corrections appearing in newspapers and magazines mostly focus on spelling errors and misreported titles, dates, affiliations, attributions, and other facts and figures printed in error. Just about every major news publication runs a corrections box, noting reporting errors and making them right. "That's not only a matter of simple fairness," state *New York Times* editors in describing the importance of reporting corrections in their newspaper, "but also because corrections enhance our credibility."(16)

If you have been involved in an interview, and the resulting story has a factual error that you believe should be corrected, contact the reporter to let him or her know. The reporter may feel slightly embarrassed but should not take it personally. Keep your discussion to the point. There should be no need to get angry. Mistakes happen, although I think it is amazing how relatively few occur considering the volume of information published in major newspapers and magazines. The *New York Times* reports that on an average weekday, it "contains nearly 130,000 words of news, information and opinion distilled from millions cascading in from throughout the world."(17)

If you do have a problem with the reporter's not recognizing the error, contact his or her editor or the publication's public editor or

ombudsman. Contact information should be noted on the corrections page, or call the publication and ask the operator for assis-
tance.

Make the distinction, though, between not liking an article
(subjective) and the misreporting of a fact (objective). You are not
going to win that battle—asking a reporter to rewrite a story the
way you would like it. There is an argument, however, for correct-
ing a story you believe was unfairly written. Don't be afraid to
stand up for what you believe is right, and keep the conversation
civil and focused on the facts. The *New York Times*, for example,
will run an "Editors' Note" to "acknowledge (and rectify, when
possible) lapses of fairness, balance or perspective—faults more
subtle or less concrete than factual errors, though often as grave
and sometimes graver." An example is "the *Times*'s failure to seek
a comment from someone denounced or accused in its columns,
or the omission of one party's argument in a controversy, resulting
from haste in fitting the article into too small a space. Or the editors may have discovered that a freelancer, assigned to review a
book, failed to divulge a conflict of interest."(18)

Misreported facts and unfair reporting used to be thrown out
with the day's paper. Their life was often short, and the frequent
advice for those injured by the mistake was to let it rest and not
give the issue more attention by seeking a printed correction.
Today, however, news lives long on the Web. Articles do not get
lost or thrown away. A misreported story stays alive in cyberspace,
and a keyword search can make it seem as fresh as the day it first
appeared.

Don't let reporting errors live on. It is important to seek corrections for an article you believe is misreported, not only to receive
a correction in print but also to accompany the article for the dura-
tion of its life on the Web.

One college took the matter in its own hands when it felt that a
local newspaper grievously misreported a story about its president.

Not receiving any satisfaction from the reporter or editor of the paper when asked to print a correction, the college posted the original article on its Web site, highlighting the reporting errors and printing the corrections.

Media Advice From Academics and Scholars

I asked a number of faculty members and institute directors with media experience for advice to other academics and scholars in their interactions with journalists. Here are some of their suggestions:

♦ Communicate complicated and nuanced ideas through example. You don't need to dumb things down; you simply need to communicate ideas clearly.

♦ The biggest difficulty for academics dealing with the media is to avoid all of the hedges that would be necessary when talking with peers. Most of us have a tendency to hedge every statement, because we are used to thinking about the boundary conditions of a particular phenomenon. Those boundary conditions often aren't at all relevant to a media story.

♦ Be incisive (advice I often have trouble taking).

♦ Only agree to speak as an "authority" on topics about which you actually have an authoritative grasp of facts/issues. Otherwise take a pass.

♦ Be aware that there is, practically speaking, no such thing as "off the record"; anything you say is liable to come back to haunt you.

♦ Don't underestimate the savvy of either the press or the public.

◆ Always remember that your goals and the goals of the reporter differ. Also, understand that the reporters rarely have in-depth understanding of the subject on which you are an expert. Simple explanations are very important. Also thinking about the misperceptions that exist is helpful.

◆ Listen well and be honest.

◆ Tell a compelling story, find an immediate news "hook" and get the message to the right people.

◆ Ditch the jargon. Connect when possible with "human interest" stories. Don't spin. Reporters really, really value talking with someone who isn't always trying to sell them a PR angle. Be willing to invest time in a relationship. Conversations are more productive than news releases.

◆ Get involved . . . in a society growing increasingly dependent on science and technology, those with expertise need to contribute to an educated/informed electorate.

◆ Control your ego/self importance. . . . Both of which can lead to "foot-in-mouth disease."

◆ If a reporter cold calls for an interview or quote, ask about the topic and tell him or her that you will call right back (they are usually on deadline). Don't be pressured. Use the interlude to think about what you want to say and compose your thoughts. Call right back.

◆ Always remain calm and level-headed. Be sure to stay within one's area of expertise.

◆ It is important to lead the media into asking better questions by suggesting topics that are also and sometimes more relevant to one's work.

- Learning/remembering: (1) Less is more. Don't offer too much beyond what is being asked. (2) Prepare. Don't simply "wing it." Know what you want to get across in advance. (3) The media are not your "friend." The media have their own agendas. (4) The media can be fair. They don't necessarily skew one's statements.

- Know what your message is, and stay on message. Be precise, keep it short.

- Don't be afraid to get your ideas out. Remember that *you* are the expert on the particular topic for which you have been contacted, and the reporter asking the questions usually wants to learn from you.

Notes

1. Pérez-Peña, R. (2009, February 9). Resilient Strategy for Times Despite Toll of a Recession. *New York Times*. Retrieved March 13, 2010, from New York Times: http://www.nytimes.com/2009/02/09/business/media/09times.html

2. Zull, J. (2002). *The Art of Changing the Brain: Enriching the Practice of Teaching by Exploring the Biology of Learning*, p. 129. Sterling, VA: Stylus.

3. Larry Summers on the Economy. (2008, April 03). Retrieved January 3, 2010, from *On Point With Tom Ashbrook*: http://www.onpointradio.org/2008/04/lawrence-summers

4. Hilton, J. (1990). *Be Prepared!* pp. 47–48. Champaign, IL: Sagamore Publishing; Morrison & Tyson Communications. *Media Interview Tips*; Penn State Department of Public Information. *Tips on Working With the Media*.

5. Heher, A. (2008, July 10). Obama Accepts Jackson's Apology for Crude Remark. Retrieved January 3, 2010, from the *Boston Globe:* http://www.boston.com/news/politics/2008/articles/2008/07/10/obama_accepts_jacksons_apology_for_crude_remark/

6. Bush Tells Crowd at GOP Fundraiser "Wall Street got Drunk." (2008, July 23). Retrieved July 23, 2008, from *USA Today*: http://blogs.usatoday.com/ondeadline/2008/07/bush-tells-crow.html

7. Safire, W. (1989, October 29). On Language; Off the Record. Retrieved January 3, 2010, from the *New York Times*: http://www.nytimes.com/1989/10/29/magazine/on-language-off-the-record.html?scp = 1&sq = on%20language%20off%20the%20record&st = cse

8. Lanson, G., & Stephens, M. (1994). *Writing & Reporting the News* (2nd ed.), p. 226. New York: Oxford University Press.

9. On Deep Background. (1994, December). American Journalism Review. Retrieved May 12, 2008 from http://www.ajr.org/article.asp?id = 1621

10. Buckley, C. (2008, March 16). A Monster of a Slip. Retrieved January 3, 2010, from the *New York Times*: http://www.nytimes.com/2008/03/16/fashion/16samantha.html?_r = 1&scp = 1&sq;eqa%20monster%20slip&st = cse

11. Mott, G. F. (1958). "First Catch Your Rabbit." In G. F. Mott and others (Eds.), *New Survey of Journalism* (4th ed.), pp. *189–191*. Barnes and Noble.

12. Lamb, B., & Mudd, R. (2008, April 6). *Roger Mudd, Fmr. CBS Correspondent & Author—Part II*. Retrieved January 9, 2010, from Q & A: http://www.q-and-a.org/Transcript/?ProgramID = 1174

13. Lanson & Stephens, *Writing & Reporting the News*, p. 240.

14. Crichton, M. (1996). *Airframe*, pp. 109–110. New York: Knopf.

15. Iannone, C. (2008, August 11). A Critic in Full: A Conversation With Tom Wolfe. *Academic Questions*, 21(2).

16. Hoyt, C. (2006, May 10). Q&A on the Time's Correction Policy. Retrieved January 9, 2010, from the *New York Times*: http://publiceditor.blogs.nytimes.com/2006/05/10/qa-on-the-timess-correction-policy/?scp = 1&sq = q&a%20on%20the%20times's%20correction%20policy&st = cse

17. Hoyt, C. (2009, January 18). Leaps of Faith, and the Trouble That Followed. Retrieved January 9, 2010, from the *New York Times*: http://www.nytimes.com/2009/01/18/opinion/18pubed-web.html?_r = 1&scp = 1&sq = Leaps%20of%20faith%20and%20the%20trouble%20that%20followed&st; eqcse

18. Hoyt, C. (2006, May 10). Q&A on the Time's Correction Policy. Retrieved January 9, 2010, from the *New York Times*: http://publiceditor.blogs.nytimes.com/2006/05/10/qa-on-the-timess-correction-policy/?scp = 1&sq = q&a%20on%20the%20times's%20correction%20policy&st = cse

CHAPTER TWELVE

Radio and Television Interviews

When a television or radio interview can be as short as a few seconds, getting to the point from the start is essential. Sound bites are like markers on a trail, leading the listener through the conversation. The art of encapsulating a key point in a few words and then explaining later gives you the best chance of getting the message heard. Effective sound bites often employ emotion such as humor or concern, offer an analogy, state a course of action, predict an outcome, are assertive, or they may express urgency. They grab people's attention with a few well-chosen words. They are the coin of the realm in the media.

In the 2008 Summer Olympics, 41-year-old Dara Torres, a three-time silver medal winner in swimming and the oldest swimmer ever to win an Olympic medal, was constantly interviewed by the media about her age. Her poise, confidence, and masterful use of sound bites gave her control of the conversation. "Age is just a number" or "The water doesn't know how old you are," she said with a smile.(1) The media and the audience loved it.

Here is a sampling of a few other sound bites reported by the media:

♦ "It looks like a three-dollar bill." Ernest Gilman, professor of English, New York University, quoted in *Business Week* regarding fraudulent student applications for college admissions.(2)

♦ "The rich are getting richer, but no one else is." Sandy Baum, professor of economics, Skidmore College, quoted in *USA Today* regarding high college tuition increases.(3)

♦ "I think it underscores the financial arms race that trading has become." Andrew W. Lo, director of the MIT Laboratory for Financial Engineering, quoted in the *New York Times* regarding quicker ways being developed by Wall Street to react to the news by creating more sophisticated algorithms.(4)

♦ There is a "bewildering quilt of laws in this country." Paul Gronke, professor of political science, Reed College, interviewed on Boston radio station WBUR *Here & Now* regarding early voting laws in the United States.(5)

♦ "The hotter the fire, the cooler he gets." A colleague of U.S. Treasury Secretary Henry Paulson Jr., discussing his crisis management skills in an interview on NPR's *Morning Edition*.(6)

Tighten your belt, though; the average length of sound bites seems to be continually getting smaller. A study by the Center for Media and Public Affairs found, for example, that the average length of a sound bite for presidential candidates on the network nightly news dropped to 7.3 seconds, a 26% decline since 1988

(9.8 seconds) and an 83% drop from the 1968 presidential election.(7)

As you prepare for an interview, write down the questions you believe you will be asked, as well as the ones you hope won't be, and then write your answers. Edit your responses to reach their essence. Look for sound bites. They should be clear, concise, conveying a key point or message, and void of jargon. Don't be frustrated by the process. It is not about dumbing down the conversation but offering directional points and key messages that will resonate with your audience.

Television and radio interview programs strive to be entertaining and informative. One Boston television network affiliate describes its news broadcasts as "compelling."(8) Every second counts in broadcast programming, which producers well know because audiences have the power of the remote to change to another station on a whim. To keep audience attention, broadcast hosts often introduce conflict and surprise in their interviews. Don't be caught off guard when they do it to you.

Be ready for any question that comes your way. You must be prepared. The audience will measure your response by your words, your tone, and for television, your body language. Avoid looks of surprise and anger. Be likable. Keep the audience on your side with a smile and a thoughtful response. Don't be defensive. The use of humor, analogies, and transition phrases such as "The real question is . . . ," can quickly diffuse or deflect the interviewer's attempt to put you on the spot.

In a CNN interview with presidential candidate Barack Obama, the reporter presented a laundry list of concerns regarding Obama's presidential platform. Instead of using precious air time to respond to negative questions, Obama deftly responded, "Those are old arguments, let's look at the future," and he then proceeded to present his messages of hope and change.(9) He had taken control of the interview by remaining calm, positive, and on message.

It is hard to resist a host who gives you a warm welcome off the air, prior to the interview. However, being personable and engaging does not mean the host is your friend. Once the microphone is turned on and the interview begins, it's all business. The interview may start off in an innocent fashion as the host attempts to put you at ease, but know that the tough questions are there, lined up like planes on a runway waiting to take off.

During a studio taping of a major network evening news segment, a reporter was knee to knee with the university president she was interviewing as they were perched on stools across from each other. The interviewer was friendly. She made a joke or two to lighten the mood. "Like me, trust me" is what I envisioned was going on in her mind as she easily conversed with the man I had arranged the interview for. She hoped the camera rolling in the background would be forgotten as she began her hunt for the sound bite or two that would air on the evening news.

The questions started off in a broad fashion, as she asked, What is new about this issue? Why is it important? Why should people care? Then as the president responded with specifics, she began to search for the conflict in the discussion, her tone changing from gracious host to investigative reporter. The president remained cool. He was prepared.

The reporter, not finding the sound bite she wanted, asked the president to rephrase his answer. How about saying it this way? she asked. The president smiled but was firm in his reply, that the answer he had given to her question was the most appropriate one. (See Media Interview Checklist, tip number 10 in chapter 11, p. 102, Don't let the reporter put words in your mouth.)

The interview lasted nearly an hour. The reporter repeated many of her questions, phrasing them differently each time, and it seemed she hoped the president would give her different answers. He was not worn down by her attempts. His responses remained consistent, clear, concise, and, he felt, were the best answers to the questions. He knew the interview would be edited to a few sound bites for broadcast and he did his part to make sure they would accurately reflect his views. (See Media Interview Checklist, tip number two in chapter 11, p. 102: Be prepared. Anticipate questions and develop answers that clearly state the key ideas you want to express.

Shortly thereafter, portions of the interview aired on network television. It was part of a news story about an important national issue, and the university president's 30-second segment helped frame the debate and offer a course of action. It was a successful interview for the president, and his words aired without compromise or distortion. His knowledge of the topic and preparation for his conversation with the reporter carried the day.

Not all interviews, though, start out friendly. Another reporters' technique is to begin with guns blazing. One public radio correspondent turned on his portable microphone and began firing questions while his guest, a research analyst, was still taking off his coat as he entered the room for the interview. The questions were hard hitting and meant to catch the analyst off guard and put him on the defensive. The correspondent was not neutral in the discussion, which was being taped, and appeared to have his own agenda. He was after a sound bite, it seemed, that would grab his audience and tell the story his way.

Quickly realizing the game at play, the analyst did not fall into the correspondent's trap. (See Media Interview Checklist, tip number eight in chapter 11, p. 102: Be cool. Hostile questions do not deserve hostile answers.) He smiled, removed his coat, made himself comfortable on the studio couch and calmly responded to the correspondent's questions, one by one and at a pace that was best for him. He deflected the correspondent's combativeness and accusatory tone that seemed to doubt his every answer and directed the conversation to answering questions in a positive and compelling manner. (See Media Interview Checklist, tip number 11 in chapter 11, p. 103: Formulate your response for the public. The public, not the media, is your real audience.)

Segments of the interview later aired, and the analyst was pleased with the results. His message was heard on radio stations across the county, and he had moved an important conversation to a national level of discussion.

Another option to consider when faced with tough questions is to run down the clock on the time allotted for your interview. Politicians are masters of this approach. Vice presidential candidate Sarah Palin's technique to maneuver out of a tough spot in an interview was to repeat her words. This was "her way of running down the clock as her mind searches for where she wants to go," said John Bitney, policy director for her campaign for governor and her chief debate coach.(10)

Interviews are two-way conversations. Take shared control of the flow and direction of the discussion. Present your key messages. Repeat them so the audience will remember what they are. Use transitional phrases to steer the discussion. Common refrains include: "The point I want to make . . . , I think another important issue to discuss is . . . , That is a good question, another is . . . , Let me summarize what I think are the key issues." Listen for words or phrases the interviewer says that allow you to link your responses to your key messages. See the conversation as presenting multiple opportunities to tell your story.

Don't wait for the interviewer to guide you through the discussion hoping he or she will ask you all the right questions. They may never get to them or know what they are, and achieving your goals for the interview may be missed. You are the expert on the subject being presented. Be prepared to introduce early in the interview, whether directly or through the use of transitional phrases, what you believe are important points for the discussion. They can set the direction for the interview and allow time for elaboration and summary.

End strong. Leave the audience and your host with your key message. "Thank you for inviting me on your show," says the guest who then says as the interview about climate change comes to a close, "I appreciate this opportunity to discuss the critical need for the U.S. Congress to develop a stronger alternative energy program for America."

Take time to study the art of giving a good interview. Watch programs like NBC's *Meet the Press*, CBS's *Face the Nation*, and some of the popular cable talk shows. See how the pros handle interviews, answering tough questions and presenting key points. What is their body language telling you? Listen to NPR and other radio interview formats. What sound bites resonate with you during interviews and news segments?

Television Interview Basics

One's body language and appearance on television can mean as much or more to an audience than the words spoken.

What to wear. Become familiar with the program. How does the host dress? How about the guests? What do they generally wear? For most television programs, appropriate dress usually means a professional look as opposed to casual. Avoid wearing bright white, red, all white, or all black colors, clothing with intricate or small patterns, or a lot of jewelry. The camera does not respond well to these colors, styles, and distracting accessories. For men, wear dark socks that reach mid calf or higher. A charcoal gray jacket or suit is a good color choice. For women choosing to wear a skirt or dress, go with a length that you do not have to tug at to keep it from rising higher than you are comfortable with when you are seated. If you have any questions about what to wear, ask the booker or producer who contacted you to appear on the program. Remember, you want the camera and audience to focus on you, not your clothes. Keep it simple and neat.

Body language. Be engaged with all of your body. Sit up straight, no slouching, as I saw one college president do as she seemingly disappeared into her chair while being interviewed on PBS by journalist Charlie Rose. Avoid a lot of hand gestures and bouncing around; it is distracting to viewers. Don't sit with your arms folded across your chest; in body language terms, this says keep out. Look at the person talking to you, not at the camera. Don't be afraid to smile. Let the host and audience like you. Smiling can also help release body tension. Respond to the conversation with appropriate facial expressions. Nervous smiling, however, when discussing serious issues can be disconcerting to viewers.

Body language can tell an audience more about a person than what he or she says. In a *USA Today* interview with Dan Hill, an expert in facial coding, a system that classifies facial movements, he described what the facial expressions of the 2008 presidential candidates might tell us.

John McCain forces smiles and, true to his reputation, angers easily as demonstrated by puffed cheeks and a chin thrust upward in disgust, Hill says. Hillary Clinton smirks, an expression "she oddly enough shares with President Bush," which conveys an attitude of assurance bordering on superiority and smugness. Barack Obama has the best true smile, but flashes it rarely for someone who speaks of hope, and Hill sees flashes of disdain, aloofness, disappointment and exasperation.(11)

A social psychologist who studies nonverbal communications said that "people often believe the nonverbal signs over what is being said."(12)

Speech. Speak up. No "ums" and "ahs." Don't let your sentences trail off with your words fading at the end. Be conversational; don't use stilted language or jargon. Take a breath between responses; don't race through your sentences. Randy Sparks, associate professor of marketing at the University of Dayton, whose research focuses on the art of persuasion, finds that "People are very, very concerned about the style of the message. Style [specifically, the fluency of one's speech and the confidence in presenting oneself] has a strong impact on whether you are persuaded." Sparks said that "the degree to which a speaker is fluent has an effect on his or her credibility. Even though what someone says may make sense, you are more likely to think they don't know what they're talking about" if they are not fluent.(13)

Tucker Carlson, former host of CNN's *Crossfire*, sums up learning the media basics as being pretty simple. His advice? "Don't wear white, show up sober, and try to speak in complete sentences."(14)

Notes

1. Thomas, K. (2008, August 18). Guiding Athletes in Spotlight's Glare. New York Times, p. D1.

2. Porter, J. (2008, August 28). U.S. Colleges Stumped by Fraudulent Applications. Retrieved January 9, 2010, from *Business Week*: http://www.businessweek.com/bschools/content/aug2008/bs20080828e960253.htm

3. Grynberg, N. (2008, September 3). Less Affordable Colleges May Get "F," Land on Wall of Shame. Retrieved January 9, 2010, from *USA Today*: http://www.usatoday.com/news/education/2008–09–03-tuition-affordability_N.htm

4. Arango, T. (2008, September 14). I Got the News Instantaneously, Oh Boy. Retrieved January 9, 2010, from the *New York Times*: http://www .nytimes.com/2008/09/14/weekinreview/14arango.html

5. Gronke, P. (2008, September 18). Early Voting. Retrieved January 9, 2010, from *Here & Now*: http://www.hereandnow.org/2008/09/show-run down-for-9182008/

6. Garten, J. (2008, September 29). *Wall Street Bailout Heavy on Paulson's Shoulders*. Retrieved January 9, 2010 from National Public Radio: http://www.npr.org/templates/story/story.php?storyId=95157373

7. *Sound Bites Get Shorter*. (2000, November 11). Retrieved March 27, 2008, from PR Watch: http://www.prwatch.org/node/384

8. 7NEWS. (2008). Boston, MA: WHDH TV (from a commercial).

9. Obama, B. *Presidential Forum on National Service*. Atlanta, GA: CNN (from a TV interview).

10. Seelye, K. (2008, October 1). Past Debates Show a Confident Palin, at Times Fluent but Often Vague. *New York Times*, p. A20.

11. Jones, D. (2008, February 24). It's Written All Over Their Faces. Retrieved January 10, 2010, from *USA Today*: http://www.usatoday.com/ money/companies/management/2008-02-24-ceo-faces_N.ht m

12. Rizvi, T. (2008, October 8). *Unspoken Message*. Retrieved January 10, 2010, from the University of Dayton: http://news.udayton.edu/News _Article/?contentId=18724

13. Shindell, C. (2008, September 26). *Persuading Talk*. Retrieved January 10, 2010, from the University of Dayton: http://news.udayton.edu/News _Article/?contentId=18508

14. Parker, A. (2008, October 26). At Pundit School, Learning to Smile and Interrupt. Retrieved January 10, 2010, from the *New York Times*: http:// www.nytimes.com/2008/10/26/fashion/26pundit.html?_r=1&scp=1&sq =At%20Pundit%20School,%20Learning%20to%20Smile%20and%20In terrupt.%20%20&st=cse

CHAPTER THIRTEEN

Opinion Articles

O ne of the quickest ways to create or advance national dialogue
about an issue important to you is by writing an opinion
article for a major newspaper, magazine, or news Web site.
It can be the most direct, meaningful, and safest (you are the one
telling the story) media option you can employ. The opinion pages
are generally among the most read sections of a publication. In
2008 the *Wall Street Journal* announced it was adding a third full
page of daily opinions to the newspaper.(1) Realizing this solid
reader interest, and no longer limited by page size because of the
Internet, many newspapers and magazines are also featuring
expanded opinion sections on their Web sites. The *New York
Times*, for example, launched "Instant Op-Ed," which allows the
paper to post immediate expert viewpoints on breaking news.(2)
Media's demand for well-written and timely opinion articles is
increasing.

Opinion articles are often confused with editorials and sometimes even with letters to the editor. Each is distinctively different.
Simply stated, editorials are the views of the publication and are

written by staff writers. Opinion articles, or op-eds as they are commonly referred to because they run opposite the editorial page, represent the views of readers and contributors about important and timely topics. They are generally between 600 and 800 words in length and are not written in response to editorials or columns, which can also be on the op-ed page. They are not about how a reporter covered a story or a response to other op-eds that have appeared in a publication. These are all topics for letters to the editor. As one former major newspaper editor told me, op-ed authors are normally people whose opinions and ideas have a special claim on our attention because of their expertise or role in decision making. Letters submitted by readers are much shorter than opinion articles and are expected to state their position with only a point or two.

An excellent example of the power of an opinion article to introduce new ideas and have a meaningful impact on public discourse is an essay written by Robert Zemsky, education professor and chairman of the Learning Alliance for Higher Education at the University of Pennsylvania. His piece, "Have We Lost the 'Public' in Higher Education?" appeared in the *Chronicle of Higher Education*.(3)

Zemsky's research revealed a growing market influence on higher education, and he was concerned about the limiting effect this was having on colleges' and universities' capacity to serve their public purposes and fundamental missions. To advance this important discussion in higher education and with the public, he met with a group of editors and writers at the *Chronicle of Higher Education* in Washington. This presentation of issues and ideas led a *Chronicle* editor to ask Zemsky to write an opinion for the newspaper's Review section. The 3,070-word piece appeared in print and on the *Chronicle*'s Web site. Zemsky quickly received readers' responses to the essay, and a national discussion had begun.

Among those who read the essay was Marlie Wasserman, director of Rutgers University Press. Wasserman e-mailed Zemsky saying she was impressed with the article and thought that there had to be a book in there somewhere. That correspondence led to the publication of *Remaking the American University Market Smart and Mission Centered*. A key part of the volume was excerpted in the *Chronicle*.(4)

A Texan named Charles Miller who also read the *Chronicle* article contacted Zemsky and invited him to attend a gathering of academic leaders and scholars in Colorado to discuss pressing issues facing higher education. This meeting was a precursor to the federal Commission on the Future of Higher Education, which Miller headed and Zemsky was asked to join. His views, as expressed in his opinion article, became part of the national discussion, as policy makers and academic leaders shaped future federal policy recommendations affecting higher education.

Zemsky's *Chronicle of Higher Education* articles and status as a commissioner generated more national media interest. Reporters increasingly recognized him as an expert source to call on for their articles and broadcast interviews about higher education issues. A new book offer followed, and Zemsky began writing a blog for the *Chronicle* in which he created a discussion community, addressing important issues facing higher education.

Another example of the power of the opinion article in reaching mass audiences and broadening awareness about a topic is Scott Reynolds Nelson's essay "The Real Great Depression." Appearing in the *Chronicle of Higher Education*, it "generated a huge amount of media attention around the world," as well as in "Wall Street investors looking for guidance," the *Chronicle* reported. A history professor at the College of William and Mary, Nelson "has been featured by *The New York Times* and public radio station WNYC, and he has been interviewed by newspapers in Greece and

New Zealand. The article has been translated into Italian, Korean, and Russian."(5)

Approaching the Opinion Page Desk

Each news outlet responds differently to opinion article submissions. Most require a fully written essay before they will give your story consideration. If your article is in response to breaking news or if the publication requires longer pieces, the editor may be willing to discuss your thoughts for an article over the phone or review a letter of inquiry that introduces your topic, key points of discussion, and your expertise in the subject. What you may learn with an initial phone call or letter to the opinion desk is that you are on the right track and the door is open for you to proceed further. An editor may even offer some suggestions on what he or she would like to see addressed in an article. This is only the first step, though, and it is no guarantee your piece will appear. That will be determined only after the opinion desk editors have reviewed your completed work.

Should you choose to call someone on the opinion desk to gauge interest in a topic for an essay, be prepared to get to the point immediately and make a persuasive argument for the importance and timeliness of the piece and the issues you would address. As in your writing, base your conversation on facts, not emotion, and avoid all jargon. You may be given a minute or two to tell your story, but it could begin a rapport with an editor and give you a direction for following up.

Here is an example of how a call to an opinion desk might go:

Hello, my name is Jane Doe and I am a professor of economics from Thoreau College and author of the book *Economics for a*

New Century. I am calling to ask if (name of publication) would be interested in considering an opinion article on the topic of the economic fallout of the housing market crash. More families in the United States will be losing their homes than any time since the Great Depression, and the federal government, if it acts now, can break this cycle of foreclosures. The article I am proposing would look at the options that the government and home owners have and recommend a course of action that may prevent more devastating losses to families and bring the U.S. economy out of a recession.

Opinion editor's reply 1. "Yes. Sounds interesting. Please send your article to my attention and we will review it and get back to you." (Great. You're on first base and now have a contact for follow-up.)

Reply 2. "No, thank you. We have just commissioned a piece on a similar topic." (Good to know, saves you time in writing something that conforms to this publication's requirements and waiting for a reply, which would have been "No, thank you." It is possible too that the editor will say no to your piece but suggest a related topic that would be of interest to him or her.)

Reply 3. "Thank you for calling, but we won't know if we are interested until we read your article." (Fair enough. You may want test the waters elsewhere, though, checking with other publications to gauge their interest.)

Another approach, and the most common, is to write an article and send it in unsolicited. In 2004 the *New York Times* received "roughly 1,200 unsolicited submissions" every week.(6) Around this time, *USA Today* received "as many as 100 to 150 submissions a week,"(7) and the *International Herald Tribune* totaled "about 200 each week."(8) In 2003 Newsweek's "My Turn" received "more than 500 manuscripts every month, and only four or five can be published."(9)

Your article, along with a brief letter of introduction presenting the issue you are writing about and your credentials, can be sent to opinion desks by e-mail, fax, or U.S. mail. When using e-mail, I recommend that the article be sent as an attachment and included in the body of the e-mail, following your introduction. This allows your recipient a choice, should he or she be hesitant to open an attachment in an unsolicited e-mail as a precaution against introducing computer viruses.

If you send your opinion article by e-mail to a news outlet, you will usually receive an automatic reply confirming receipt and giving a timeline for review. Generally, you will receive a response in a week or two. If you have not heard from anyone in this time period, you can pretty much assume the publication is not interested.

Keep in mind that the more popular the publication, the more competition you will have in attempting to place your article. If you have a particularly time-sensitive essay, that is, in a few days or a week or two the issue you are writing about will have become old news, it makes sense to start with an outlet you think offers the best chance of success in publishing your piece. This may mean choosing a regional newspaper over a national one because of the better odds of acceptance. Here again, a phone call to the opinion page editor may deliver a quicker response. However, when your topic is not as time sensitive, reach high if you think your article is worthy. This may mean starting with the *New York Times* or the *Wall Street Journal* and, if required, work down a priority list of outlets to approach.

Keep in mind that national newspapers and magazines require an exclusive, as do most or all of the major regional publications, and they will not accept an article that has appeared elsewhere. You need to approach these outlets one at a time when submitting your article.

Op-Ed Format

Opinion articles for popular media such as the *New York Times*, *USA Today*, *Wall Street Journal*, and *Newsweek* vary in length. The *Times* takes submissions of 650 words, *USA Today* opinion articles range from 650 to 750 words, the *Journal* prefers 600 to 1,200 words, and *Newsweek*'s "My Turn" essays are between 850 and 900 words. As for the educational press, the *Chronicle of Higher Education,* for example, takes essay submissions for its Review section that are between 1,000 and 1,600 words, or about four to seven double-spaced typed pages. *Inside Higher Ed* accepts articles between 1,000 and 2,000 words. Most outlets list submission guidelines on their Web sites.

Articles should be typed, double spaced, and include your name, title, institution, physical address, day and evening telephone numbers, and e-mail address. Even though editors will most likely change it should your article appear, a headline that pulls the reader into the story should also be provided. "A headline that does not arouse interest at first glance fails its purpose," said George Fox Mott in *New Survey of Journalism.*(10)

Op-Ed Writing Style

The writing style for an opinion article is pretty constant. Make your point at the beginning, present a strong argument for your case based on facts not emotion, avoid jargon, and recommend a course of action. The *International Herald Tribune* advises writers submitting opinion articles to

> open with a clear sense of what you're writing about and why the reader should care about it, then continue with a cogent argument leading to a strong conclusion. Too many articles give a great

description of the problem, but then peter out into [a] feeble conclusion that "it's high time" somebody does something. Give us a forward-looking and original solution. . . . Don't wait too long. News quickly goes stale.(11)

Former *New York Times* deputy editor Susan Lee's rules of the "Op-Ed page game" for would-be contributors, cited in Edwin Diamond's *Behind the Times*, include, "Do not be too complicated, or too sophisticated [when writing an op-ed]. Newspaper readers do not want to pause while they are reading. . . . The simpler the ideas, the better."(12)

New York Times op-ed page editor David Shipley, in a 2004 *Times* article titled, "And Now a Word From Op-Ed," said, "The Op-Ed editors tend to look for articles that cover subjects and make arguments that have not been articulated elsewhere in the editorial space. If the editorial page, for example, has a forceful, long-held view on a certain topic, we are more inclined to publish an Op-Ed that disagrees with that view."

Other qualities the *Times* looks for in an op-ed, he noted, are "timeliness, ingenuity, strength of argument, freshness of opinion, clear writing and newsworthiness."

Does it help the odds of your article being selected if you are famous? "Not really," Shipley said. "In fact, the bar of acceptance gets nudged a little higher for people who have the means to get their message out in other ways. Op-Ed real estate is too valuable to be taken up with press releases."(13)

Writer George Earley recommended in a piece he wrote for *The Writer* titled "Writing the Op-Ed Article" that "once you feel sufficiently familiar with your target market to be able to write for it [i.e., you are writing for the reader not the editor], find a topic that's of strong interest to you. The op-ed page is an opinion page; if you aren't strongly interested in your topic, it's going to show in your writing and you'll swiftly get a rejection slip."(14)

Here are some examples of opinion article headlines and opening sentences that have appeared in major media that were written by members of the academy:

A Journey to Baseball's Alternate Universe. With the baseball season under way and the memory of scandal in the sport so fresh, many fans yearn for an earlier era, a time when mythology mingled with baseball. The sport's most mythic achievement is Joe DiMaggio's 56-game hitting streak, a feat that has never come even close to being matched. Fans and scientists alike, including Edward M. Purcell, a Nobel laureate in physics, and Stephen Jay Gould, the evolutionary biologist, have described the streak as well-nigh impossible. *New York Times. Written by Cornell graduate student Samuel Arbesman and professor of applied mathematics Steven Strogatz.*(15)

NE Must Tackle Problem of a Worsening Climate. This winter has been a strange one—periods of extreme cold followed by unseasonable warmth. While some may consider this a "good old fashioned winter," it bears little resemblance to those of the 1950s or '60s. Scientists and policymakers alike are concerned that carbon dioxide emissions from burning fossil fuels are having an increasingly significant impact on our regional and global climate. *Boston Globe. Written by Barrett N. Rock, University of New Hampshire professor of natural resources and plant biology.*(16)

The Democrats' Endless Winter. In Maine, March is Mud Season. Up here, Mud Season means day after day of tinfoil sky as the snow slowly melts, revealing the oozing, saturated earth below. We get a glimpse or two of lawn before another snowstorm sweeps through, burying everything again and dashing any hopes that winter will soon end. . . . On the national political stage, it's Mud Season as well—a time of attack ads, a time of questioning character. These are the days of "red phone" commercials, of plagiarism accusations, of assertions that "hope" is just a four letter word." *New*

York Times. Written by Colby College professor of English Jennifer Finney Boylan.(17)

Why We're Still Happy. These days, bad news about the economy is everywhere. So why aren't we panicking? Why aren't we spending our days dejected about the markets? How is it that we manage to remain mostly preoccupied with the quotidian tasks and concerns of life? Traffic, dinner, homework, deadlines, sharp words, flirtatious glances. Because the news these days affects everyone. *New York Times. Written by University of California, Riverside, professor of psychology Sonja Lyubomirsky.*(18)

One last thought about writing style: "Be concise, but not brief," said executive development consultant Roger Flax in an article he wrote for the *TWA Ambassador* about effective writing skills. "Many people think that 'concise' and 'brief' represent the same thing, but they don't. 'Concise' means saying it in as few words as possible and getting to the point. 'Brief' means keeping it short. Your message should be as short as possible, but thorough and complete. Eliminate all unnecessary words."(19) Amen.

Op-Ed Added Value

A college president once wrote an opinion article that never appeared in print but directly led to his being interviewed on PBS's *MacNeil/Lehrer NewsHour* (with Robert MacNeil's departure from the newscast in 1995, the program's title changed to the *NewsHour with Jim Lehrer* and then to *PBS NewsHour* as it is know today) and NPR's *All Things Considered.*

He wrote about the Clinton administration's National Service initiative that was just being announced, and he was offering his perspective as a college president about its national importance. I was attempting to place the article for him, and it was always "under consideration" by one outlet or another. In the meantime, though, I presented the article to *NewsHour* and *All Things Considered*, suggesting it as a base for an interview with the author. It was all there for the producers to consider, 600 words of a well-presented argument for the support of a national student service policy. It validated the college president's expertise on the issue and offered a framework for the television and radio interviews that took place.

The exercise of writing the opinion article, and the research that went into this piece, also positioned the president among his peers, alumni, and other key audiences to become a leading voice on this important national issue. The article was never printed in a major publication (thought it probably found a home in the college's alumni magazine), but it undoubtedly was well worth the president's effort to write it. Opinion articles, in a number of ways, are valuable documents in shaping discussion and advancing dialogue. They are your words presented in a context you believe to be important. And, as *USA Today* editors recommend, if your opinion article is not accepted by them, "You may want to consider recasting your thoughts in a letter to the editor and resubmitting them to our letters column."(20)

Notes

1. The New Opinion Pages. (2008, April 21). *Wall Street Journal,* p. A16.

2. Strupp, J. (2008, December 19). New York Times to Launch "Instant Op-ed." Retrieved December 19, 2008, from *Editor & Publisher*: http://www.editorandpublisher.com/eandp/news/article_display.jsp?vnu_conte nt_id = 100392377. Media Post News. (2008, December 19). NYT to Launch 'Instant Op-Ed.' Retrieved March 13, 2010, from http://www.mediapost.com/publications/index.cfm?fa = Articles.sho wArticle&art_aid = 97040]

3. Zemsky, R. (2003, May 30). Have We Lost the "Public" in Higher Education? *Chronicle of Higher Education,* 49(38), p. B7. Retrieved January 10, 2010, from http://chronicle.com/article/Have-We-Lost-the-Public-i/21529/

4. Zemsky, R., Wegner, G., & Massy, W. (2005, July 15). Today's Colleges Must Be Market Smart and Mission Centered. *Chronicle of Higher Education,* 51(45), p. B6. Retrieved January 10, 2010, from http://chronicle.com/article/Todays-Colleges-Must-Be-Ma/35802/

5. Winkler, K. (2008, October 31). When the Chronicle Published an Essay on the Financial Crisis, Wall Street Listened. *Chronicle of Higher Education.* Retrieved January 10, 2010, from http://chronicle.com/article/When-The-Chronicle-Publishe/41880/

6. Shipley, D. (2004, February 1). And Now a Word From Op-Ed. Retrieved February 2, 2004, from the *New York Times*: http://www.nytimes.com/2004/02/01/opinion/01SHIP.html?pagewanted;eqprint&position =

7. Walte, J. Letter from *USA Today* editor/columns (personal communication).

8. More information about opinion articles. (2005, December 29). Retrieved February 3, 2008, from the *International Herald Tribune*: http://iht.com/articles/2005/12/29/opinion/web.opinfo.php

9. Cooper, N. (2003, August 11). Letter from Newsweek "My Turn" editor (personal communication).

10. Mott, G. F. and others (1958). Headlining the News, from Mott, G. F. and others (Eds.), *New Survey of Journalism* (4th ed.), p. 225, Barnes & Noble.

11. More information about opinion articles.

12. Diamond, E. (1993) *Behind the Times,* p. 279. New York: Villard.

13. Shipley, And Now a Word From Op-Ed.

14. Earley, G. (1985, March). Writing the Op-Ed Article. *The Writer,* p. 14–15.

15. Arbesman, S., & Strogatz, S. (2008, March 30). A Journey to Baseball's Alternate Universe. Retrieved January 17, 2010, from the *New York Times*: http://www.nytimes.com/2008/03/30/opinion/30strogatz.html

16. Rock, B. (2004, March 15). NE must tackle problem of worsening climate. Retrieved January 17, 2010, from the *Boston Globe*: http://www.boston.com/news/globe/editorial_opinion/oped/article s/2004/03/15/ne_must_tackle_problem_of_a_worsening_climate/

17. Boylan, J. (2008, March 23). The Democrats' Endless Winter. Retrieved January 17, 2010, from the *New York Times*: http://www.nytimes.com/2008/03/23/opinion/23boylan.html

18. Lyubomirsky, S. (2008, December 26). Why We're Still Happy. Retrieved January 26, 2010, from the *New York Times*: http://www.nytimes.com/2008/12/27/opinion/27lyubomirsky.html

19. Flax, R. (1991, September). Do the Write Thing. *TWA Ambassador*, pp. 37–41.

20. Walte, J. Letter from USA Today editor/columns (personal communication).

CHAPTER FOURTEEN

Letters to the Editor

Within that 6-by-15-inch letters box on the editorial page, space is coveted because it's one of the more favored features, better read even than some Page One stories," wrote *Boston Globe* ombudsman Jack Thomas (a member of the news staff who represents the newspaper's readers). "A *Globe* survey," he went on to say, "found that letters were perused by 52 percent of readers, which means they have a larger audience than do most columnists."(1)

Letters to the editor are the response of readers to articles or editorials appearing in a newspaper or magazine. Small in size, they are a powerful means to advance discussion on important issues. And, as one *New York Times* editor said to me, the letters section is a place where writers and editors find new sources for their stories.

New York Times letters editor Thomas Feyer in an article to readers said that letters "come in relentlessly, round the clock from around the country and around the world, at a rate of roughly a thousand a day. My small staff and I try to read them all but we can publish only about 15 letters a day."(2) The *Washington Post* each week receives "approximately 1,400 letters to the editor and all of them are read." About 70 of them make it to the letters to the editor page.(3)

Editors will admit that the selection of letters is "highly subjective," as Feyer wrote. Sharing some insight into what *Times* editors look for in their selection of letters for publication, he offered the following thoughts: "We are looking for a national (and often international) conversation about the issues of the day—big and not so big—as well as fresh, bright writing that stands out through its own charm. Timeliness is a must; brevity will improve your chances; stylishness and wit will win my heart." He warns, though, "Letter writers . . . are entitled to their own opinion, but not to their own facts."(4)

San Francisco Chronicle editorial page editor John Diaz echoes the importance of word length. "I think the strongest letters are often among the shortest," he wrote to readers in an article titled, "What Makes a Good Letter to the Editor?"

> Sometimes letters get passed over because they resemble a ransom note with a smattering of boldface words and capitalizations to emphasize their VERY IMPORTANT POINTS. Let the power of your prose and your arguments carry the day, not the caps lock on your keyboard. This goes for punctuation too!!!!!

Another insider's guideline Diaz offered his readers is that the *Chronicle* copy editors "screen out letters that are too personal in tone or engage in gratuitous name calling."(5)

Offering a five-part approach to writing a letter to the editor, the *New York Times* provided the following outline, which appeared on its letters page:(6)

Title:
A Letter to the Editor
1. Introduction
   Restates the thesis of the original article.
2. Opinion
   Supports/contradicts the writer's point.
3. Anecdote
   Relates relevant personal experience.
4. Evidence
   Cites an independent study, report, etc.
5. Conclusion
   Restates the opinion of the letter writer.
   Signed,
   A. Reader

Timing is critical, and waiting a week to send a letter in response to a news item or event you read about in the paper is too late. The immediacy of e-mail has accelerated the submission cycle. The *Times* tells its readers that "writing by the next day is a good idea."(7) A *Washington Post* tip for getting your letter published is to "be among one of the first to send us comments on a current issue or event."(8)

Each publication has its own requirements for the word length of letters it will accept. The *New York Times* recommends that letters be kept to about 150 words.(9) *USA Today*'s maximum length is 250 words.(10) The *San Francisco Chronicle* asks submissions to its letters page be limited to 200 or fewer words.(11) Study the letters page of the publication you're planning to send a submission to. The letters you see are the winners in this competition for coverage. Get a sense of their style and format.

Your letter should be exclusive to the publication receiving it. It can be sent by e-mail (preferred because of timing), fax, or U.S. mail (so the news outlets say, but it seems like a slow way to get there when there are quicker options available). Include your name, title, institution, home and e-mail addresses, along with your daytime and evening telephone numbers. Contact information often is listed on the letters page of a publication or on its Web site. Also, you can call the media outlet to ask for this information.

Notes

1. Thomas, J. (1999, April 12). How to get your letter into the Globe: Patience, skill, and luck help. *Boston Globe*, p. A15.

2. Feyer, T. The Letters Editor and the Reader: Our Compact, Updated. *New York Times*. Retrieved March 14, 2010, from the *New York Times*: http://www.nytimes.com/2004/05/23/opinion/23READ.html?scp = 1&sq = the%20lette rs%20editor%20and%20the%20reader%20our%20compact %20updated&st = cse

3. News & Editorial, Frequently Asked Questions. *Retrieved February 15, 2008, from the Washington Post*: http://washpost.com/faq.nsf/0/ 207ED6260E2A3C3885256BA0006B44AF?OpenDocument&News_Ed

4. Feyer, *The Letters Editor and the Reader: Our Compact, Updated.*

5. Diaz, John. (2000, January 30). What Makes a Good Letter to the Editor? *San Francisco Chronicle*, p. SC-1. Retrieved January 26, 2010, from http://articles.sfgate.com/2000-01-30/news/17636043_1_letters-editor-section-memo

6. *New York Times*. (2005, July 17). Essay Test: The Young and the Terse (4 Letters). Retrieved January 26, 2010, from http://www.nytimes.com/ 2005/07/17/opinion/l17educ.html?scp = 1&sq = essay%20te st%20the%20 young%20and%20the%20terse%204%20letters&st = cse

7. Feyer, T. (2003, September 14). *To the Reader:* The New York Times. Retrieved March 14, 2010, from the New York Times: http://www.nytimes .com/2003/09/14/opinion/to-the-reader.html?scp; eq1&sq = thom as%20 feyer%20september%2014%202003&st = cse

8. *News & Editorial, Frequently Asked Questions.* The Washington Post. Retrieved February 15, 2008, from the Washington Post website: http:// washpost.com/faq.nsf/0/207ED6260E2A3C3885256BA0006B44AF?Open Document&News_Ed

9. Feyer, *The Letters Editor and the Reader: Our Compact, Updated.*

10.Walte, J. (1995). Letter from John Walte, editor/columns. *USA Today.*

11. *San Francisco Chronicle.* Guidelines for Submissiion the The San Francisco Chronicle. (2003, March 7). Retrieved March 7, 2007, from http://www.sfgate.com/chronicle/submissions/

CHAPTER FIFTEEN

Speeches

When I asked the dean at one of the top ten business schools how he determined the ranking of other business schools, particularly those not in his tier, when he fills out the annual *U.S. News & World Report* "America's Best Graduate Schools" survey, he said it was often based on which institutions' faculty were giving presentations or moderating panels at the major business school conferences he attended during the year.

For him, it was a quick validation of which institutions and individuals were active in their fields, respected by their peers, and presumably doing good work.

Media professionals think the same way. When they are looking for expert sources to call upon for their stories, a quick way to learn who the top people in a field are is to see who is presenting work at the major professional conferences. They know the process is not an exact science, and one can be a speaker at a conference and not be a leader in his or her field, but it is a good place to start, particularly when you need information fast, as reporters do.

Delivering a major speech or heading an important panel discussion at a national conference also presents an opportunity for the speaker to contact the media. The conference signals the presence of new ideas and discussions that could be of interest to the media for stories and interviews.

You will often see, for example, a stream of science reporting in the media, nationally and internationally, about new research and important issues being presented at the annual meeting of the American Association for the Advancement of Science (AAAS).

The AAAS annual meeting "is a major attraction for the scientific, business, NGO [nongovernmental organizations], media, and policy-maker communities concerned about the interaction of science and technology with society."(1) It is an event that provides a venue for speakers and the issues they discuss to receive wide media attention.

The theme for the AAAS 2009 Annual Meeting was "Our Planet and Its Life: Origins and Futures." The association recognized 2009 as the 200th anniversary of Charles Darwin's birth and the 150th anniversary of the publication of his book *On the Origin of Species by Means of Natural Selection*. Major coverage of key presentations was reported around the world.

Smaller professional events also prompt media coverage. A college president delivering a talk to a lunch gathering of 100 student loan company representatives about serving low-income students generated a national story written by an enterprising reporter who was in attendance. The newspaper article led to further public and media interest. Foundation representatives and college and student loan professionals contacted the president's office for copies of his address. This lunch guest speaker quickly became a key source for the media and others regarding the issue of best practices in the student loan industry.

Plenty of good advice about delivering an effective speech is available in bookstores and on the Web. The communications office for an institution, organization, or one's professional society also may provide helpful guidance. Though the focus of academic presentations can be all about the data, knowing basic presentation techniques helps build an attentive audience.

Here is excellent advice from the pros in the business of helping people become better public speakers, Toastmasters International:

1. Know your material.
2. Practice. Practice. Practice!
3. Know the audience. Greet some of the audience members as they arrive.
4. Know the room. Arrive early, walk around the speaking area and practice using the microphone and any visual aids.
5. Relax.
6. Visualize yourself giving your speech.
7. Realize that people want you to succeed.
8. Don't apologize for any nervousness or problem.
9. Concentrate on the message—not the medium. Focus your attention away from your own anxieties and concentrate on your message and your audience.
10. Gain experience. Mainly, your speech should represent you—as an authority and as a person. Experience builds confidence, which is the key to effective speaking.(2)

Another piece of advice I've found helpful is to focus on individuals throughout your audience. Do not constantly scan the room as you give your speech, with your head moving from side to side as though you were watching a tennis match. Connect with your audience by delivering one full thought to a person or small group and then to another. It is more personal, helps control your anxiety, and allows for more visual feedback from your listeners.

A popular tip for delivering an effective speech that I find helpful to remember is:

1. Tell them what you are going to tell them.
2. Tell them.
3. Tell them what you have just told them.

That is, repeat your key points. Some writers will tell you that the average length for memorable phrases in a speech is about six words. This is evident in America's presidential inauguration addresses: "To bind up the nation's wounds," Abraham Lincoln; "A thousand points of light," George H. W. Bush; "Begin again the work of remaking America," Barack Obama.

The recommended optimal length for a speech is 20 minutes. In a *Wall Street Journal* article titled "Critics Are Succinct: Long Speeches Tend to Get Short Interest," one public-speaking adviser said this regarding the preferred length of a speech: "If you can do it in 20 minutes, you have the best shot at the minds of the people present. Sixty minutes is suicide. You should commit it—or they will."(3)

Check well in advance on upcoming professional conferences in your field. Each may present an opportunity for you to contact the organizer and offer to deliver a presentation on your area of expertise or to serve as panel moderator. Once on board, work with the organizers in their media outreach efforts. Let them know you are available for media interviews, and give them possible topics of news interest that you can discuss as they relate to the theme of the conference. If you have been keeping up with the news as we discussed in chapter 3, offer the conference organizers names of people in the media you know or believe would be interested in your topic for discussion and whom they might contact in advance of your presentation.

The value of a speech can last well beyond the event in which it is delivered. It can serve as excellent background to send to media covering your field. If your speech is more than a few pages, send the media a CliffsNotes version with an offer to provide them with the full text. It may prompt the media to cover the issue or call upon you as a story source on related topics. Use your speech as the base for an opinion article. Take its core ideas and put them in a context that a reader of a newspaper, trade publication, or professional journal might be interested in. Send your speech or a summary of it to talk radio programs that you would feel comfortable appearing on, suggesting it as a base for an interview and offering yourself as a guest.

Make speeches part of your agenda, and make the most of them when you do. Some conference organizers provide book signing opportunities for keynote speakers. Most publishers are more than happy to supply the organization with copies at a discount on a returnable basis, so be sure to put your publisher in touch with the organizer well in advance.

Notes

1. American Association for the Advancement of Science. (2009). *AAAS Annual Meeting Call for Symposium Proposals*. Retrieved April 18, 2008, from http://www.aaas.org/meetings/2009/program/syposia/submit/

2. Toastmasters International. *10 Tips for Public Speaking*. Retrieved January 26, 2010, from http://www.toastmasters.org/tips.asp

3. Suskind, R., & Lublin, J. (1995, January 26). Critics Are Succinct: Long Speeches Tend to Get Short Interest. *Wall Street Journal*, pp. A1, A5.

CHAPTER SIXTEEN

Book Promotion

Your job is done, so you might think. You've labored away at writing a masterpiece, and now you believe your publisher will handle the rest. You sit back and wait for the advertising, reviews, and book tours to begin. Visions come to mind of appearing on *Oprah* and *Fresh Air* with Terry Gross to discuss your book.

Unless you have a big hit on your hands, and the publisher realizes it early, you can probably count on little or none of this happening. In my experience working with academic authors and their publishers, the extent of promotion is pretty much limited to a press release sent to book review editors and a book highlight featured in the publisher's catalog. Galley proofs as they first become available may be sent to a few reviewers. Active and continued promotion of your book, however, will require your direct attention and time. And lots of it.

Lately, the news has not been great about the health of the book review section in the traditional press. Hit by unprecedented loss of newspaper advertising revenue and the downsizing of news staffs, book review sections are being eliminated in many newspapers. Former National Book Critics Circle president John Freeman wrote, "At the *Los Angeles Times*, the *Chicago Tribune*, *Newsday*, the *Minneapolis Star Tribune*, the *Memphis Commercial Appeal*, the *Cleveland Plain Dealer*, the *Dallas Morning News*, the *Sun Sentinel*, the *New Mexican*, the *Village Voice*, the *Atlanta Journal Constitution* and dozens upon dozens of other papers, book coverage has been cut back or slashed altogether, moved, winnowed, filled with more wire copy, or generally been treated as expendable."(1)

All is not lost. While the number of newspaper book sections has decreased, the number of Web sites providing book reviews and interviews with authors has grown. Blogs are the new medium that is putting books into buyers' hands. Book reviews and comments are a staple in many of these online personal journals.

Blog book tours, in which an author appears over a period of time on a string of targeted blog sites "writing guest posts, answering questions from the host or sitting for a podcast, a video interview or a live chat,"(2) has become a new industry in book promotions. According to the *New York Times*, "A blog book tour usually requires an author or publicist to take the initiative, reaching out to bloggers as if they were booksellers and asking them to be the host for a writer's online visit."(3)

Authors also take control by creating their own blogs and Web sites to build and nurture buzz about their books. An author's blog works to create conversations with the public about his or her book and issues central to the book's theme. Blogs and other book promotions such as press releases and print and broadcast interviews should direct people to the author's Web site or book page on the publisher's site for more information. Here readers can find more information about the book, the author, reviews, and links to retail booksellers such as Barnes & Noble and Amazon.

One way to create an independent blog is to approach an appropriate e-zine (online magazine or newsletter) or print periodical with a Web site to see if it might be interested in hosting or posting a link to your site. The advantage is that you can plug in to a preexisting audience with an interest in your topic, rather than build traffic from scratch. The *Chronicle of Higher Education* and *Inside Higher Ed* are two education-focused online sites that host blogs. On a local level, the *Boston Globe*, as well as other daily newspapers, features Web links to popular area blogs. Topics listed by the *Globe*'s blog index include health, politics, arts, family, and technology.

An author of children's books provides links to her biography on her Web site, games for children, information for parents and teachers, a list of her books and reviews, and book retailers where her books can be purchased. It is an interactive site designed for children, parents, and teachers. Readers return to the site for new information and activities, and each Web visit creates an opportunity for the author to sell her books.(4)

Another author, whose book is about affirmative action in higher education, welcomes readers to his Web site, letting them know at the top of his home page that "there is plenty here for scholars, journalists, and general readers, including suggestions for book discussion groups, links to additional readings and other Web sites of interest, and news updates related to the affirmative action debate."(5)

These sites are dynamic. They inform, invite reader participation, and, most important, sell books.

Another social media tool gaining traction in book promotion is Twitter. Book authors are using Twitter to post online messages and Web links about their books. These tweets, which are limited to 140 characters or fewer, allow authors to get the word out about their books and create communities interested in discussions about them. Twitter links such as thebookclub (http://www.twit ter.com/thebookclub), books_140 (http://www.twitter.com/books 140) and books_in_140 (http://www.twitter.com/booksin140) provide forums for book reviews and reader exchange. (More about blogs, Twitter, and other social media is presented in chapter 17.)

The stock in trade for promoting one's book remains the press release, which offers an overview of the book, release date, and information about the author. It names the publisher and, ideally, provides a Web link for more information. One page is the best length for your release. Sometimes media professionals will be interested in receiving a galley of your book when they learn of its being published. The *Chronicle of Higher Education*, for example, occasionally will run excerpts of a book in its *Chronicle Review* section to coincide with the book's release date.

Lists of book reviewers can easily be found on the Web through key word searches such as "book review lists." An excellent site that lists national and international print and Web book review sites, for example, is Complete-Review (http://www.complete -review.com/main/main.html). Ask your publisher for its recommended contacts. It's important to coordinate your promotional efforts with your publisher's in-house public relations unit regarding timing (you don't want to create demand before the book is in the stores or on Amazon), to ensure consistency of the message and to avoid duplication of effort.

Be persistent and methodical. Organization is the key to managing an effective book promotion campaign. Make a list of the review sites of interest to you. Share these with your publisher, as publishers routinely create review lists for new books, and allocate free copies for this purpose.

Set a schedule and a goal, sending your press release out to a targeted number of new outlets each week. Here again, work with your publisher's publicity or marketing department, as the staff may have developed a press release and a distribution list. Follow blog sites that review books or focus on issues related to your writing. Participate in the online discussions, giving readers a chance to know you and to learn about your book. Your contact list should be large, increasing your odds for success. Be prepared for a long journey. It can be a frustrating process but worth the effort. Publicity is the strongest tool you have to generate public interest in the purchase of your book.

One noted author, speaking from experience, advises people not to put energy into book tours and readings. Contrary to what one might think, these events do not necessarily sell books he said. People attending may be interested in seeing the author, but this does not translate into book purchases. Tours and readings, however, do allow authors to make friends with the book store managers hosting the events. These individuals can be instrumental in promoting the sale of an author's book. One independent bookseller emphasized in a radio interview that she is a "bookseller and wants to get an author sold."(6) Success, it seems for most authors, as one writer said, is niche marketing. For him, this translated into getting to know independent booksellers.

Other means to get the word out is to contact media outlets that report on areas relevant to your book. If you are writing about the stock market, you might contact investment reporters and bloggers. If your subject is climate change, make a list of environmental reporters to get in touch with. Let them know about your book and the issues presented that relate to their area of reporting. Offer to serve as a story source for their articles.

Follow the news. It is common to see authors of new books writing opinion articles for major newspapers, magazines, and news Web sites about timely events in which their expertise and knowledge of the topic directly relate to the issues relevant to their book.

One author of a new book about race, class, and education access wrote an opinion article that appeared in *USA Today* on the Republican presidential candidate's views about affirmative action.(7) An author of a book about terrorism and national security wrote an opinion article for the *Wall Street Journal* in which he referred to the 50th anniversary of Senator Joseph McCarthy's starting his televised hearings on alleged spies and communists in the U.S. Army. This was his news hook to write about McCarthy's abuse of power and presenting his folly as a lesson for modern times.(8) And an author of a book about evolution wrote an essay for the *Chronicle of Higher Education* in which he presented some of the mysteries of the human genome.(9)

Authors also are asked to be contributing writers to various publications, writing articles that relate to the topics of their books. Authors can work to create these opportunities by contacting editors of news sections in which these commissioned articles appear and suggesting story ideas. A newspaper weekend feature section or magazine is a good outlet to approach, for example. The *Boston Sunday Globe*'s Ideas section featured a front-page article by a Penn State University historian and author on the history of Christianity, which was the theme of his new book.(10)

If you are presenting a paper at a professional or scholarly conference, check whether your publisher will be exhibiting, and if so, its staff would probably be willing to arrange a book signing at the company's booth.

As all publishers always stress, whenever you write an article or make a presentation on the topic of your book, make sure that the book's full title (and, if possible, the publisher's name) is included in the accompanying bio or acknowledgment.

Letters to the editor are often overlooked as a way for authors to be heard and to generate buzz about their books. These relatively short missives, some being 125 words or fewer, elicit reader attention both from the public and the news outlet publishing them (see chapter 14). In this case, the author of a letter to the editor would address an issue presented in an article that is germane to his or her book. It's a good idea to add the word "author" to your signature along with the title of the book. The name of the author of the letter is always printed, and sometimes additional information is kept when the letters page editor believes it adds credibility to the views expressed.

Interviews with guest authors are an essential component for many talk radio programs. NPR, Public Radio International, and Voice of America host a series of excellent talk shows that regularly feature interviews with authors of new books. Check these and other radio Web sites to find a listing of programs, which name the hosts and offer contact information. Find the shows of interest to you. Listen to them. Get a feel for each host's interview style. Contact the programs you like, sending your press release and book reviews to each show's host or producer, saying you would welcome the opportunity to be an on-air guest.

As for television, the catch-22 for book authors is that it often takes coverage to receive coverage on one of the networks or cable stations. Landing an interview on television pretty much requires first having a lot of early buzz about your book. It needs to be recognized in reviews and articles as interesting reading. A well-placed opinion article in a leading publication like the *New York Times* also could get you noticed, generating a call from a TV booker or producer. *The Oprah Show, Charlie Rose, The Daily Show with Jon Stewart*, and *The Colbert Report*, the morning network talk shows, along with C-Span's *Book TV*, are among those programs that make up the current A-list of interview options for many authors.

Just as you need to ensure that your book's title appears in a print article, you need to ensure that your book's title is mentioned as least twice during a radio or television interview. If your host doesn't give the title when introducing you, be sure to do so yourself at the first appropriate opportunity ("As I say in my new book . . ."). TV hosts are usually good about showing the audience the interviewee's book on the program. To be on the safe side, bring a copy of your book to the interview.

College and university Web sites offer opportunities for book reviews. The communications offices for these institutions are always looking for good Web content and book reviews, which may be written by a communications staff member and are popular postings. Realizing the "declining opportunities for coverage of faculty books in traditional media," The University of Texas at Austin began ShelfLife@Texas, a blog developed by the university's Office of Public Affairs that is dedicated to the review of books written by members of the school and its alumni.(11)

For television, as with radio, the show's producer often is the best general contact to send your cover letter, press release, reviews, and other supporting articles about your book to. Also consider sending a copy of your book to select outlets most important to you. Your budget will dictate the number of outlets this will be. The producers at C-Span's *Book TV*, for example, ask for a copy of the book when approached for a review. Your publisher should be more than willing to provide a free copy for this purpose.

If you can't find a show's contact information on its Web site or through a telephone call to the station, record the program. Production credits appear at the end of the show, and you'll be able to play the recording in slow motion to write down the name of the producer. Some shows that appear daily only run their credits once a week, so you will want to be aware which day this is before setting your recorder.

Remember, it takes time, organization, persistence, and luck to promote your book. This is how books are sold. When I asked one noted author for advice to fellow writers about the promotion of their books, he said, "Done right, do it yourself. No one knows more about your book than you. No one is more passionate. Authors are best at pitching their books." He added, "Relying on the publisher's in-house promotional support is naive. The worst advice for an author to take from a publisher is 'Let us take care of the selling.'"

Notes

1. Critical Mass. (2007, April 23). *NBCC Campaign to Save Book Reviews*. Retrieved October 16, 2008, from http://bookcriticscircle.blogspot.com/2007/04/nbcc-will-fight-these-cut-backs.html

2. Jesella, K. (2007, September 2). The Author Will Take Q.'s Now. Retrieved January, 26, 2010, from the *New York Times*: http://www.nytimes.com/2007/09/02/fashion/02blog.html

3. Jesella. The Author Will Take Q's Now.

4. Rosemary Wells. Retrieved October 19, 2008, from http://www.rosemarywells.com/

5. Color and Money. *Color and Money Is a College Course!* Retrieved October 26, 2008, from http://www.colorandmoney.blogspot.com

6. Lindholm, J. (2008, December 11). *2008 Winter Reading Program*. Retrieved December 11, 2008, from Vermont Public Radio: http://www.vpr.net/episode/44993/

7. Schmidt, P. (2008, September 23). A Losing Proposition. *USA Today*. Retrieved March 14, 2010, from USA Today: http://blogs.usatoday.com/oped/2008/09/a-losing-propos.html

8. Kessler, R. (2008, April 22). The Real Joe McCarthy. Retrieved January 26, 2010, from the *Wall Street Journal*: http://online.wsj.com/article/SB120882522444233275.html

9. Barash, D. (2008, November 7). Who Are We? *Chronicle Review, 55*(11), p. B18. Retrieved January 26, 2010, from the *Chronicle of Higher Education*: http://chronicle.com/article/Who-Are-We-/26399/

10. Jenkins, P. (2008, December 14). When Jesus Met Buddha. *Boston Globe*, p. K1.

11. Howard, J. (2008, November 25). The University of Texas Gets a Litblog. *Chronicle of Higher Education*. Retrieved January 26, 2010, from http://chronicle.com/blogPost/The-University-of-Texas-Get/4401/

CHAPTER SEVENTEEN

Web 2.0 and Beyond

Mainstream media outlets are increasingly turning to the Internet for their news and story sources. Online personal journals called *weblogs* or *blogs*; social networking sites such as Facebook, Twitter, and the video-sharing site YouTube; Web audio broadcasts known as *podcasts*; and collaborative Web sites known as *wikis,* where contributors share and edit information, are fertile ground for new ideas, news, information, and public engagement.

These new media are part of the Web 2.0 phenomenon, defined as the second generation of Web-based communities and services that created online social media. They give individuals access to vast reader and viewer markets once controlled by traditional media such as newspapers, radio, and television.

Understanding the social media landscape and knowing how to enlist its use is increasingly critical to building a strong communications plan. Social media lets you reach broad audiences and allows you greater control in conveying your message. Here is a look at some of social media's essential components.

Blogs

As I write this, Nielsen BuzzMetrics, a company that tracks and analyzes online consumer-generated media, reports that the total number of blogs it has identified is now at 126,861,574, 42,234 of which are new blogs that were created in the 24 hours preceding the count.(1) In mid-December of 1997, there was arguably one, when Jorn Barger came up with the term *weblog.* (2)

A survey conducted by the Pew Research Center found that 33% of Internet users in America read blogs.(3) This number is growing in the United States and worldwide. Intel founder Gordon Moore predicted that "every eighteen months computing power will double."(4) The social media's capacity to grow seems to be unlimited.

"The power of weblogs is that they allow millions of people to easily publish their ideas, and millions more to comment on them," reports Technorati, a leading blog search engine. "Blogs are a fluid, dynamic medium, more akin to a 'conversation' than to a library—which is how the Web has often been described in the past. With an increasing number of people reading, writing, and commenting on blogs, the way we use the Web is shifting in a fundamental way. Instead of primarily being passive consumers of information, more and more Internet users are becoming active participants. Weblogs allow everyone to have a voice," notes Technorati.(5) *Business Week* calls blogs "a free form of publishing."(6)

Faculty have been quick to embrace this new medium. Go to a college or university Web site to see the number and variety of faculty and academic department blogs listed. Princeton University has its blogs about politics(7); the University of California, Berkeley, has blogs on law(8); Youngstown State University has blogs on health sciences(9); and Indiana University Bloomington, has blogs about folklore and ethnomusicology.(10) The diversity of topics is vast, and the media are paying attention.

"Historically, scholars might develop a reputation as public intellectuals once they become senior statespeople in their fields; increasingly, younger researchers are using blogs as resources for reputation building, especially in cutting-edge fields that lack established authorities," said Henry Jenkins, of the University of Southern California. Jenkins, who is the Provost's Professor of Communications, Journalism and Cinematic Arts and former co-director of the Massachusetts Institute of Technology's Comparative Media Studies program, is "often called the Marshall McLuhan of our day" according to the *Chronicle of Higher Education.*(11) "Historically, academics have been put in a reactive position, responding to questions from reporters. Blogging places academics in a more proactive position, intervening more effectively in popular debates around the topics they research," Jenkins said.(12)

According to Technorati,

> Bloggers are often sources for journalists, and many blogs contain commentary and riffs on what journalists wrote that day. Frequently, newsmakers use blogs to respond to what journalists write about them. And by linking to traditional media, weblogs can introduce new readers to journalists and their publications. . . . The relationship between blogging and journalism can be characterized as symbiotic rather than competitive.(13)

Newspapers and other media sites have begun to link readers to independent blog sites. The *Boston Globe* features bloggers who are not on the newspaper's staff who write about the arts, computers and technology, politics, media, and a host of other topics.(14) Thomas Litwin, director of Smith College's Clark Science Center, kept readers of the *Globe's* environmental blog, The Green Blog, posted on his activities when he and other scientists were on board a U.S. Coast Guard cutter collecting environmental data in the Bering Sea. Litwin said he wrote the blogs because he wanted "to start a conversation with readers" about the scientific work being done to better understand the ecosystem of this area. "In the Lower 48 we don't think much about the fact that we are an Arctic nation having seasonally ice-covered international borders. This is also a place where the scientific and political worlds live side by side," he wrote.(15)

Robert Scoble is a noted blogger who writes about technology and is coauthor of *Naked Conversations: How Blogs Are Changing the Way Businesses Talk With Customers*. He provides readers of "Scobleizer" with a "Corporate Weblog Manifesto," in which he presents his "ideas of things to consider before you start" a blog.(16)

Some of his suggestions are

1. Tell the truth.
2. Post fast on good news or bad.
3. Use a human voice. [I would add: Avoid the use of jargon and write in a conversational style. An internal *Washington Post* memo addressing blog guidelines for news staff states that what works are blogs with voice and a consistently strong (even provocative) writing tone.(17)]
4. Make sure your system supports the latest software/Web/human standards. If you don't know what the W3C is, find out [World Wide Web Consortium]. If you don't know what RSS feeds are, find out [Really Simple Syndication, a Web feed providing frequently updated information]. If you don't know what weblogs.com is, find out. [Weblogs.com is a

"server that automatically notifies subscribers when new content is posted to a website or blog."(18)]

5. Have a thick skin.
6. Talk to the grassroots first. Why? Because the mainstream press is cruising weblogs looking for stories and looking for people to use in quotes. People trust stories that have quotes from many sources.
7. If you screw up, acknowledge it. Fast.
8. Never change the URL on your weblog. I've done it once and I lost much of my readership and it took several months to build up the same reader patterns and trust.
9. If your life is in turmoil and/or you're unhappy, don't write.
10. If you don't have the answer, say so. Not having the answer is human. But, get it and exceed expectations. If you say you'll know by tomorrow afternoon, make sure you know in the morning.
11. Never lie. You'll get caught and you'll lose credibility that you'll never get back.
12. Never hide information.
13. If you have information that might get you in a lawsuit, see a lawyer before posting, but do it fast.
14. Link to your competitors and say nice things about them.
15. Be the authority on your product/company [or an authority in your field]. You should know more about your product than anyone else alive, if you're writing a weblog about it. If there's someone alive who knows more, you damn well better have links to them. [Point taken, although this is not always the case when dealing with academic disciplines and areas of research. It is OK not to be the absolute authority in your field, if one even exists. But you should be one of them if you are writing a blog on a particular topic.]

Arguments can flare up on blog sites like wildfire. A good tool to help keep the discussion productive and civil is to direct readers to respected third-party sites that provide added context on the topic. You are the moderator, so keep your cool and promote a healthy and vibrant discussion among participants on your blog.

Starting a blog is easy. A Web search on the topic will list many online sites where you can create your own blog and find advice for developing, maintaining, and promoting it. A service I used, which is free and owned by Google, is Blogger (http://www.blog ger.com). In fewer than five minutes, I was easily able to create my own site and begin blogging. Steps included creating a Google account, choosing a name for my blog, entering an e-mail address, and selecting a page template (i.e., how the page will look) among the many options provided.

But before you jump in and start blogging, have a plan. Ask yourself: What are my goals? What will I write about? Who is my audience? How much time will I commit to posting new blogs and responding to reader comments? Twice a day? Once a week?

Maintaining consistency in posting, more than frequency, is essential to a successful blog. Don't overcommit yourself. More is not necessarily better; content matters most. If what you are writing is important to readers, they will adjust to your posting schedule. However, if they have to guess when your next post will be, you risk losing them. If your postings are too infrequent, though, they may forget about you. Find your comfort level and stick to it.

I once did a small survey of blogs written by college presidents. The overwhelming pattern for most of the sites was that the blogs started off strong. They had a sense of adventure, mission, and fun in their writing. The presidents had a lot to say and were posting once or twice a week. Soon the newness faded. Within a few weeks, postings dropped, and issues presented seemed less important. Within the year, postings went from once or twice a week to monthly and sometimes longer. Readers who returned to these sites, I am sure, could tell that these blogs became a distraction and a chore for the presidents. Instead of casting a dynamic light on their offices, the inconsistency of the blogs worked against them. The initial goal of creating a vibrant blog community was gone.

A few key steps can get your blog off and running. First, tell your friends and colleagues; send them the Web address, or URL, in an e-mail. It's an easy way to start a dialogue with readers and begin to hone your blogging skills. If they like the site, chances are they will tell their friends and colleagues about it as well. Next, participate in blog communities on topics similar to yours. "You need to begin your online publishing career by socializing in established online communities related to your 'beat.' Writing about politics? Keep a diary at *Daily Kos*, blog at *RedState*, submit to *Huffington Post*, or hang out in the *TPM* Café," advises Robert Niles, editor of the Annenberg School of Journalism's Online Journalism Review.(19)

Post frequently if you have something meaningful to say. Google tracks how often your site is updated. Frequent postings increase your site's ranking. The higher the number, the better the chance that others will find your site. "Faculty members could blog a couple of paragraphs about their work just once a week—thoughts, helpful resources, an interesting article or book, a short summary of their latest ideas—which would dramatically increase their 'Google rank,' since search engines give preferential rank to blogs," says Scott McLeod, director of the Center for the Advanced Study of Technology Leadership in Education at Iowa State University.(20)

Make your post headings concise and interesting. Like newspaper headlines, their job is to grab the reader's attention. Don't use jargon. Keep your headings short, simple, interesting, and informative. Use keywords that identify your topic and are search engine friendly. "Antarctic ice melt" would be part of my blog post title if that's what I am writing about. Think of key root words a reader might use to find your blog and put them in the title.

"Your target keywords should always be at least two or more words long," said the editors of Search Engine Watch, an online site that focuses on how Web search engines work.(21) They said that too many Web sites (and blogs) rely on a single word, such as "education," to define themselves, which places them in an overly crowded field. Two or more keywords lessen the competition and increase the odds of being discovered. "Higher education cost and quality," if that is the topic of my blog, can be a keyword phrase that breaks me out of the pack.

Besides the words in your heading, "Search engines also like pages where keywords appear 'high' on the page," according to Search Engine Watch, which recommends placing keywords in the headline and in the first couple of paragraphs of your Web page.

Increase your link popularity. Find the leading blog sites relevant to yours. A Google blog search can quickly list the top sites related to your key word parameters. Contact other bloggers and ask if they will link to your site. Treat these calls or e-mails to blog authors the same as you would your contacts with mainstream media (discussed in chapter 3). Before approaching other bloggers about linking to your site, you should

- ♦ be familiar with the blog and the author you are about to contact. Part of making a good first impression is letting the author know you've participated on his or her site.

- ♦ have a concise description of your blog and why it could be a meaningful link for the author to add to his or her site.

Having other bloggers link to your site can increase the Web ranking of your blog. Bloggers like linking to other interesting blogs because it makes their site more useful and dynamic for readers. Those in the mainstream media are finding this out and have begun to link their sites to outside Web sites and blogs, which gave rise to the term *link journalism*. Referring to Google's mastery of linking to other Web sites, Scott Karp, head of a Web-based newswire who coined the term "link journalism," says, "It's all about sending people away, and [Google] does such a good job of it that people keep coming back for more."(22)

Twitter

The next step in blogging is Twitter, "the microblogging sensation," as *Business Week* calls it. "People use it to send tiny haiku-like messages (140 characters maximum) to everyone who chooses to receive their feeds."(23) As it seems with many new social media developments, Twitter's meaning in our lives will catch up to our use of it. Many people may not immediately grasp the relevance of tweeting, thinking, "What a waste of time." However, social media quickly has a way of proving the naysayers wrong.

Twitter.com is in its early stages but is quickly going viral around the world. Its popularity has grown by millions since it started in 2006. Built around the question, "What are you doing now?" Twitter is a social networking service that allows you to create a forum for discussion as well as track others and respond to their tweets on your cell phone or the Web, "reaching millions of users instantly," according to Twitter (www.twitter.com). "The site offers a quick way of reaching like-minded folks and gathering information," says Jay Rosen, a New York University journalism professor and avid blogger.(24)

Not just a "thing" for teenagers as many people perceive it to be,(25) the applications of Twitter range from posting about the banality of one's daily life: "I'm getting pizza for lunch," to creative uses of social networking such as astronauts tweeting from space to keep their followers posted on events as they orbit the Earth(26); church goers being prompted by their pastors to tweet throughout their services, "encouraging people to integrate text-messaging into their relationship with God"(27); and researchers forming Twitter groups to stay connected on shared projects. Secretary of State Hillary Rodham Clinton has even touted Twitter's "great diplomatic potential."(28)

Media are adopting Twitter in news gathering and reporting. They are posting tweets, asking their followers for news sources and story ideas. Reporters post updates on breaking news and developments, creating a form of Twitter journalism. "Twitter entries build a community of readers who find their way to longer articles because they are lured by these moment-by-moment observations," said John Dickerson, chief political correspondent for *Slate*.(29)

Media luminaries such as NBC's *Meet the Press* host David Gregory, ABC's *Nightline* co-anchor Terry Moran, and CNN's *Newsroom* anchor Rick Sanchez post messages to their followers on Twitter.com. The Web site Muck Rack (http://www.muckrack .com) tracks tweets from reporters of the major media outlets. Another Web aggregator following the media and other categories of tweeters using Twitter is WeFollow (http://www.wefollow .com). Tracking journalists covering your field of expertise can give you added insight into their lives, current news interests, and can present opportunities for you to respond to their Twitter postings. The following is a sampling of David Gregory's tweets:

> Please send some question on swine flu for our administration officials. What is [it] you want to know???? Posted: 9 a.m., May 1, 2009.
>
> Preparing our roundtable discussion. What are your top five talkers for the week??? Posted: 9:37 a.m., May 22, 2009.

Please send some questions for our Take Two tomorrow with Doris Kearns Goodwin and Jon Meacham. Posted: 12:43 p.m., April 25, 2009.(30)

Faculty, researchers, and scholars can put Twitter to good use by joining Twitter communities of common interest and sharing information, insight, and knowledge related to their areas of expertise. If your field of study is international politics, for example, and the president of the United States is traveling to China for an official visit, your Twitter posts about the event can generate discussions and spotlight your views, such as, "I suspect China's political leaders will find the president's visit productive in building stronger economic ties between the two countries." Or let's say you're a member of a research team out at sea studying the summer migration of humpback whales in the North Pacific. You can send daily tweets keeping all who are interested posted on your findings and observations.

Media professionals follow Twitter postings, looking for new conversations, insight, and sources on important news topics. Twitter postings allow you to make references to your research, articles, and books and to provide Web links that offer more information about them. As with other methods of communicating with the public, such as opinion articles, letters to the editor, and blogs, Twitter offers a new medium worth exploring. Its difference, in part, is in its immediacy. It provides "super fresh"(31) information and can allow real-time conversations in the Twitter community, which is 75 million and counting.(32)

Twitter Basics

Becoming a member of Twitter.com is simple, and it only takes a few minutes to register and begin sending tweets. A search function allows you to easily find Twitter postings of interest by entering a person's name, topic, geographic location, phrases, and more. Twitterers tend to make their conversations public rather than private, although keeping your tweets limited to an individual or small group is optional. "Nearly 90 percent of Twitter users make their updates public, so everyone can read them," reported *USA Today*.(33)

Twitter Terminology

Social media has its own language. Here are some of the basic terms that the Twitter community employ:

Twitterers: members of the Twitter.com community.

Tweets: Twitter posts containing 140 characters or less that can be read on a computer or cell phone. Twitter counts all letters, punctuation, numbers, symbols, and spaces as characters. Tweets appear in reverse chronological order on your viewing page. *Re-tweets*: passing along what someone else wrote on Twitter.

Tweeps: people following your postings.

Hashtag: search engine coding, keywords preceded by the pound sign (#). Using a hashtag is an efficient way to group tweets about the same topic, which can be easily found using search.twitter.com. For example, entering "#energy research" into Twitter's search function will produce all the postings on this subject.

Web Sites

Make it easy for the media to find you on the Web. As with blogs, media professionals are combing Web sites for new ideas, sources, and story information. "I use websites to get story ideas, to identify sources, to learn context," says *Inside Higher Education* editor

Scott Jaschik in a *University Business* article about how the Web can help generate media coverage.(34)

What makes a good Web site? Scott McLeod, director of the Center for the Advanced Study of Technology Leadership in Education at Iowa State University, offers the following advice in a techLearning blog titled "The Importance of Being 'Clickable'":

> Assuming that academics want to have their work better known (and thus used), there are a few basic steps that would significantly increase their visibility. The first step would be for faculty to expand their department Web pages. Instead of merely listing their degrees, contact information, and courses, faculty could list their publications and their abstracts, post slides from their conference presentations, and upload copyright-protected drafts of working papers, all of which would give Internet search engines more information to index.
>
> Second, faculty could hyperlink to the journals and to the organizations that publish their work so that visitors could easily access them.
>
> Third, using wikis with their classes could create resources that benefit not only their students but also other audiences across the globe.
>
> Finally, faculty members could blog a couple of paragraphs about their work just once a week: thoughts, helpful resources, an interesting article or book, a short summary of their latest ideas which would dramatically increase the "Google rank," since search engines give preferential rank to blogs. They also would realize immeasurable gains from their colleagues subscribing to, and commenting upon, what they post. (35)

McLeod warns that "academics who don't take advantage of these new tools risk obscurity, and thus irrelevancy. As well, they miss out on substantial personal and professional benefits."

Take, for example, Harvard professor Mahzarin Banaji's Project Implicit. "When Mahzarin R. Banaji created a Web site to advance her scholarly research on prejudice, she had no idea it would become a cultural phenomenon," reported the *Chronicle of Higher Education*.(36) Banaji, now a professor of social ethics in the Department of Psychology at Harvard University, created her Web site 10 years ago as part of her research on prejudice while teaching at Yale University. "She was simply looking for bodies to take a few tests." Richly adding to her research and advancing public discourse, Banaji's Project Implicit reports that "visitors have completed more than 4.5 million demonstration tests since 1998, currently averaging over 15,000 tests completed each week."(37)

The media also are paying attention to Banaji's Web research, with coverage about Project Implicit appearing in the *New York Times*, *Washington Post*, *Wall Street Journal*, *Newsweek*, *Time*, and *Psychology Today* and on NBC, the Discovery Channel, CNN, and more, nationally and internationally.

Wikis

Wiki communities can be found on just about any topic of shared interest, and as with blogs and tweets, those in the media find them to be a rich source of new ideas and story contacts. A wiki allows users to post and edit Web page content, similar to working in a Microsoft Word document. The most famous wiki is Wikipedia, the online encyclopedia that can be viewed and modified by volunteers worldwide.

Popular Web sites for the creation and hosting of wikis are PBwiki, Wetpaint, and Wikispaces. The world's largest provider of hosted business and education wikis, PBwiki hosts over 400,000 wikis and serves millions of users per month.(38) Tutorials on how to create an effective wiki are offered on these and other hosting sites.

The national association Educause, which focuses on the effective use of information technology in higher education, states in its primer, "7 things you should know about . . . Wikis," that "the first wikis appeared in the mid-1990s. Scientists and engineers used them to create dynamic knowledge bases. Wiki content—contributed 'on the fly' by subject-matter specialists—could be immediately (and widely) viewed and commented on. Adapted as an instructional technology in the past few years, wikis are being used for a wide variety of collaborative activities."(39)

Podcasts

Podcasts are professional or homemade broadcasts available on the Internet.(40) A grassroots form of radio, the number of podcasting listeners has climbed from about 12 million in 2006 to nearly 18 million in 2008.(41) These audio or video files can be downloaded free from the Internet to a computer or portable audio player. Listeners can subscribe to podcasts that are then automatically delivered to their systems. A number of programs used to download podcasts are available, such as Apple's iTunes, a popular choice among podcast listeners.

According to *Macworld*, the computer magazine, "Podcasting is amateur radio at its best: people from all around the world are recording their own broadcasts on topics ranging from technology to religion. Listeners subscribe to the broadcasts, which are downloaded to iTunes or to an iPod for listening on-the-go."(42) iTunes is a free software application for Macs and PCs. An iPod is a portable media player (in tech years, a distant descendant of the transistor radio); the smallest currently has 4 GB of storage, can hold 1,000 songs (or tons of podcasts), and is a little shorter than the length of a standard house key.

Podcasts, whose name is said to derive from *iPod* and *broadcasting*, "can be audio files, video files, documents or any combination of the three," according to Apple. "Any television or radio program can be transmitted as a podcast, as can any lecture, performance or other recorded event."(43) The primary distinction between a podcast and downloadable audio is the ability to subscribe to them," said Shel Holtz, author of the book *How to Do Everything with Podcasting*.(44) Listeners can subscribe to podcasts by using a Web format such as RSS (Really Simple Syndication) or XML, to feed regularly changing Web content to their systems.

Many faculty are podcasting their courses for students and others to download. Colleges and universities are featuring faculty expert podcast series such as The Johnson School at Cornell University. Each month, the business school notes, a faculty member is interviewed on his or her research and oftentimes asked to offer insight into a current news event as it applies to the person's area of expertise.(45) For example, a Johnson School professor of investment management was interviewed about the causes of the subprime mortgage crisis.

Like other social media, podcasts serve as another means to deliver your message to a wide audience, including to the media that follow podcasters related to their field of news coverage. The technology is easy to use. According to Apple, "In 12 minutes and 31 seconds, you can start podcasting."(46) Costs for software and equipment (a microphone and headphone hooked to your computer) are minimal. Apple's GarageBand is a popular audio recording and editing program used by podcasters.(47) Miniature video cameras like Flip's Mino (48) fit into a shirt pocket, cost not much more than $100, connect to your computer's USB port, and enable you easily to record interviews or live events, and post them on the Web. The Flip Mino comes with its own editing software that's easy to use. You can also post videos to YouTube (see p. 180).

Starting and maintaining a successful podcast series, however, takes time, commitment, scheduling, and most of all, having something to say. Essential questions to ask yourself before venturing into podcasting are, "What is my story?" and "Why should somebody (i.e., a listener) care?" A professor of environmental studies may want to begin a podcast series that focuses on climate change research, policy, and change strategy. A director of a peace and social justice program may want to talk about current societal concerns and actions for redressing them.

Podcast Format

Good advice offered by GarageBand support for structuring a podcast includes

- ◆ Shoot for a show length of 20 to 30 minutes.

- ◆ Keep topics moving, and limit topic coverage to 5 to 8 minutes. [Determine the key message(s) for each topic you want to leave with your audience.]

- ◆ Try to use guests as a way to break up the conversation, pace, and tone of your shows.

- ◆ Use musical backgrounds (known as jingles) or other non-musical interludes as transitions between topics. These topic breaks are typically described as bumpers or sweepers, giving your listeners the time they might need to digest the content you just presented.(49)

Promoting Your Podcast

Some key steps to take for promoting your podcast are

1. Establish your delivery system. Create an account for your podcast on FeedBurner (www.feedburner.com). This is an easy-to-use free software service from Google that does all the legwork (coding, management of information) to allow listeners to subscribe to your podcasts through Web feeds such as RSS, XML, and Atom. Feeds are a way for Web sites to distribute content. They "permit subscriptions to regular updates, delivered automatically via a Web portal, news reader or e-mail."(50)

2. Describe your show. Use keywords, or *tags*, which identify your topic and are search engine friendly. Provide a description that is concise and interesting. It is your advertisement and is designed to elicit reader attention and interest. This root information describing your podcast is referred to as *metadata*.

   Example:

   Name of program: Earthwatch Radio.

   Tags: Environment, Science, Climate Change, Talk.

   Description: "Earthwatch Radio is a series of two-minute programs on environmental issues and scientific research. It is produced by the University of Wisconsin–Madison by the Gaylord Nelson Institute for Environmental Studies and the Sea Grant Institute."(51)

3. Post a link to your podcast on your blog or Web site. Include the metadata for the show and a description of the current episode. Note that your blog and podcast can be complementary—each offering content for the other at great efficiency.

4. List your podcast on multiple podcast directories. At last count, there are over 160 free podcast services to select

from.(52) These services index your podcast based on the information you provide and make it available to the public. Popular directories include iTunes, Podcast Alley, Podcast Directory, and podCast411. iTunes, for example, currently lists 64,599 podcast sites and 4,308,280 episodes.(53)

A quick and easy way to become listed on a variety of podcast directories is to use Google's free directory notification service, PingShot. It will automatically inform Web aggregators, search engines, and directories when your content is updated. To access it, click on the Publicize tab of the FeedBurner application.(54)

5. Send out a press release. Write a release (see chapter 5) about your podcast and send it to the media covering these issues. Online press release services will list your press release free, such as i-Newswire (http://www.i-newswire.com) and PR-inside (http://www.pr-inside.com). Paid news distribution services, which send your release to media outlets around the country and beyond, include PR Newswire (http://www.pr newswire.com) and Ascribe (http://www.ascribe.org).

6. Participate on blog and podcast sites related to the theme of your podcast. Establish your expertise on the issues presented. Let fellow participants know about your podcast, and provide a link to it.

Podcasts can be a great way to inform an audience about issues important to you, create communities focused on these topics, and promote learning and action. Beyond adhering to basic podcast rules in production and format, the quality of content, that is, having a story to tell, determines the success of a show. Remember: "If it doesn't resonate in the offline world, it won't resonate in the online world."(55)

YouTube

"YouTube produced more hours of video in the past six months than the three major networks have produced since 1948," said a scholar of social media.(56) Launched in December 2005, You-Tube, a free online video sharing service, had 95 million unique viewers and 6 billion total streams (real-time Internet sound or video) during the month of May 2009.(57)

This social media behemoth is so powerful and user friendly it became a fundamental communication tool in Barack Obama's presidential campaign. Realizing its ability to reach millions of potential voters, the staff at BarackObama.com uploaded more than 1,800 videos to their candidate's YouTube site.(58) Continuing to marshal the phenomenal social connectivity of the site, Obama's current YouTube profile reads:

Joined: September 05, 2006.
Last Signed In: 1 day ago.
Subscribers: 175, 221.
Channel Views: 21,893,029.
Party: Democratic.
Current Office: President.(59)

Academics and scientists are discovering YouTube's value in getting heard. As a PhD candidate, inventor Johnny Chung Lee posted a five-minute video on YouTube "that became an Internet sensation," reported the *New York Times*.(60) The video (61) focused on Chung's research in video technology and the eye-popping virtual reality desktop display he developed.

It caught people's attention. Microsoft wanted to hire him. His head-tracking video has been downloaded over seven million times so far.

"Contrast this with what might have followed from other options Mr. Lee considered for communicating his ideas," the *Times* reported. "He might have published a paper that only a few dozen specialists would have read. A talk at a conference would have brought a slightly larger audience. In either case, it would have taken months for his ideas to reach others."(62)

Lee has been named one of the top young innovators in the country, and he credits much of his success to his postings on YouTube.(63) "Sharing an idea the right way is just as important as doing the work itself," he said. "If you create something but nobody knows, it's as if it never happened."(64)

An increasing number of faculty members are posting their lectures on YouTube to advance learning. At Penn State over 30% of its faculty say YouTube plays a role in their teaching.(65) Campuses across the country are posting videos of faculty lectures and talks on their institutional home page and YouTube site.

The late Randy Pausch, who had been a professor of computer science at Carnegie Mellon University, delivered a now famous "last lecture" that was videotaped and posted on YouTube. His lecture, a legacy to his life and the lessons he learned, gained a widespread Internet audience and has now been viewed by over 10 million people.(66)

The YouTube site for scientists, SciVee, reports that it "is changing the pace at which science is conducted and communicated." It "enables scientists to make their research more visible, shareable, and accessible throughout the research cycle."(67) By allowing researchers to post accompanying video with their research papers, a goal of SciVee is the "widespread dissemination and comprehension of science."(68)

YouTube makes it easy to get started posting videos. Tutorials and tips about video production and uploading are offered on the YouTube Web site, accessible by clicking on the Handbook link at the bottom of the home page (http://www.youtube.com). Your institution's communication office should also be able to assist you in your YouTube production.

Techniques for getting the word out about a YouTube production are similar to those used for promoting other social media sites such as blogs and podcasts: Use keywords or tags that identify your topic and are search engine friendly. Tell your friends and colleagues. Include YouTube links on your blog and Web site. Participate in social media communities, letting them know who you are. Share your expertise and interests, directing people to your YouTube site.

Facebook

Make it easy to be found. With more than 400 million active users and nearly 1 million new members signing up each day, Facebook "is rapidly becoming the Web's dominant social ecosystem and an essential personal and business networking tool in much of the wired world," states the *New York Times*.(69) Originally designed as a social networking site for college students, Facebook's fastest growing demographic today is people 35 years old and older.

Register on Facebook (http://www.facebook.com) and complete a profile, listing your expertise and areas of scholarly interests. You can post links to your Web page, blog, tweets, YouTube videos, journal articles, and more. Keep it professional. Reporters use social networking sites like Facebook to find story sources.(70) This is your calling card or billboard for journalists and others whom you would like to inform about your work and connect with on a professional level.

The obvious warning: Don't post information that could embarrass you. If your intent is to advance discussion and learning about important issues, stay on message. Resist trying to blend your professional presentation with the personal details and photos meant for friends and family that are frequently included in Facebook profiles.

"Effective new tools for social media are becoming available constantly and can be useful in reaching specific audiences," said Jeffery Hanna, executive director of communications and public affairs at Washington and Lee University. "Combining tools—and finding applications that allow these combinations—is especially useful. For instance, many new applications allow you to update your blog, your Facebook page and your Twitter account all at the same time. That not only represents a time-savings but it also permits you to stay on message."

Notes

1. BlogPulse. (2008, May 1). *BlogPulse Stats*. Retrieved from http://blog pulse.com/index.html

2. Wortham, J. (2007, December 17). After 10 Years of Blogs, the Future's Brighter Than Ever. *Wired*. Retrieved December 5, 2009, from http://www.wired.com/print/entertainment/theweb/news/2007/12/blog_anni versary

3. Smith, A. (2008, July 22). New numbers for blog readership. Retrieved April 16, 2010 from Pew Internet & American Life Project: http:// pewinternet.org / Commentary / 2008 / July/New-numbers-for-blogging-and-blog-readership.aspx

4. Leyden, P. (1997, May). Moore's Law Repealed, Sort Of. Retrieved January 26, 2010, from *Wired*: http://www.wired.com/wired/archive/5.05/ ff_moore.2.html

5. Technorati. *Blogging Basics*. Retrieved March 30, 2008, from http:// support.technorati.com/support/siteguide

6. Baker, S., & Green, H. (2008, June 2). Beyond Blogs. *Business Week*, pp. 045–050.

7. McCarty, N. (2009, October 9). *My Prediction for the Nobel Prize in Economics*. Nolanmccarty.com. Retrieved December 3, 2009, from the Princeton University website: http://blogs.princeton.edu/mccarty/

8. Berkeley Law. *Blogs*. Retrieved December 3, 2009, from http://www.law.berkeley.edu/2270.htm

9. Barefoot, M. *Health Sciences Blog*. Retrieved December 3, 2009, from Youngstown State University: http://maagblog.ysu.edu/healthsciences/

10. Jackson, J. *Jason Baird Jackson*. Retrieved December 3, 2009, from http://jasonbairdjackson.com/

11. Jenkins, H. (2008, April 4). Public Intellectuals in the New-Media Landscape. *Chronicle of Higher Education, 54*(30), p. B18. Retrieved January 26, 2010, from http://chronicle.com/article/Public-Intellectuals-in-the/16203/

12. Jenkins, H. (2008, April 4). Public Intellectuals in the New-Media Landscape. *Chronicle of Higher Education, 54*(30), p. B18. Retrieved January 26, 2010, from http://chronicle.com/article/Public-Intellectuals-in-the/16203/

13. Technorati, *Blogging Basics*.

14. *New England Blogs*. Retrieved December 5, 2009, from the *Boston Globe*: http://www.boston.com/community/boston_area_blogs/

15. The Green Blog. (2008, March 31). Into the Ice: An Exploration of the Bering Sea at the Dawn of Global Warming. Retrieved January 26, 2010, from the *Boston Globe*: http://www.boston.com/lifestyle/green/greenblog/2008/03/thin_ice_an_exploration_of_the_3.html

16. Scoble, R. (2003, February 26). *The Corporate Weblog Manifesto*. Retrieved from Scobleizer: http://scoble.weblogs.com/2003/02/26.html

17. Dube, R. (2007, November 5) *Washington Post blog guidelines*. Retrieved March 29, 2008, from CyberJournalist.net: http://www.cyberjournalist.net/news/004477.php

18. Weblogs. Retrieved March 11, 2009, from http://weblogs.com/about.html

19. Niles, R. (2008, April 25). *How do I get people to come to my website?* Retrieved January 26, 2010, from Online Journalism Review: http://www.ojr.org/ojr/stories/080425niles-promotion/

20. Baker, P. (2007, December 14). *Are you clickable?* Retrieved January 26, 2010, from Education PR: http://educationpr.org/2007/12/14/are-you-clickable/

21. Sullivan, D. & Bruemmer, C. (2007, March 14). *Search Engine Placement Tips*. Retrieved January 26, 2010, from Search Engine Watch: http://searchenginewatch.com/2168021

22. Stelter, B. (2008, October 13). Mainstream News Outlets Start Linking to Other Sites. Retrieved January 26, 2010, from the *New York Times*:

http://www.nytimes.com/2008/10/13/business/media/13reach.html?_r=1&
pagewanted=print

23. Baker & Green. *Beyond Blogs*.

24. Kurtz, H. (2008, August 26). Political Coverage That's All a-Twitter.
Retrieved January 26, 2010, from the *Washington Post*: http://www.washing
tonpost.com/wp-dyn/content/article/2008/08/25/A R2008082502516.html

25. Fox, S., Zickuhr, K., & Smith, A. *Twitter and Status Updating, Fall
2009.* Retrieved January 26, 2010, from http://www.pewinternet.org/Reports/
2009/17-Twitter-and-Status-Updating-Fall-2009.aspx

26. Watson, T. (2009, May 21). In space, anyone can hear you tweet. *USA
Today*, p. 2A. Retrieved January 10, 2010, from http://www.usatoday.com/
printedition/news/20090521/nasatwitter21 . . . st.art.htm

27. Rochman, B. (2009, May 03). Twittering in Church, With the Pastor's
O.K. Retrieved January 26, 2010, from *Time*: http://www.time.com/time/
business/article/0,8599,1895463,00.html

28. Bruni, F. (2009, May 31). The world is your oyster! The sky's the
limit! These are the worst of times but you can make them the best of times.
Then again . . . *New York Times*, Week in Review, pp. 1, 4.

29. Dickerson, J. (2008, summer). *Don't Fear Twitter. Nieman Reports.*
Retrieved January 26, 2010, from http://www.nieman.harvard.edu/reports
item.aspx?id=100007

30. Gregory, D. Retrieved January 10, 2010, from http://twitter.com/
davidgregory/statuses/1670252006, http://twitter.com/davidgregory/statuses/
1884116026, http://twitter.com/davidgregory/statuses/1614986435

31. Johnson, S. (2009, June 05). How Twitter Will Change the Way We
Live. Retrieved January 26, 2010, from *Time*: http://www.time.com/time/
business/article/0,8599,1902604,00.html

32. Gaudin, S. (2010, January 26). Twitter now has 75M users; most
asleep at the mouse. Retrieved March 17, 2010, from Computerworld:
http://www.computerworld.com/s/article/9148878/Twitter_now_has_75M
_users_most_asleep_at_the_mouse

33. Graham, J. (2008, July 21). Twitter Took Off From Simple to "Tweet"
Success. Retrieved January 26, 2010, from *USA Today*: http://www.usato
day.com/tech/products/2008–07–20-twitter-tweet-social-network . . . N.htm

34. Joly, K. (2007, February). *PR on the Web 101: Institutional Public
Relations Teams May Be Preventing Their Schools From Getting Deserved
Media Coverage. Here's How the Web Can Help.* Retrieved December 12,
2009, from http://www.universitybusiness.com/ViewArticle.aspx?articleid
=679

35. McLeod, S. (2007, November 15). The Importance of Being "Clickable." Retrieved May 6, 2008, from *Tech & Learning*: http://www.techlearn ing.com/shared/printableArticle.php?articleID=196604810

36. Fogg, P. (2008, April 17). Thinking in Black and White. *Chronicle Review, 54*(46), p. B19.

37. Project Implicit. *General Information*. Retrieved March 17, 2010, from http://www.projectimplicit.net/generalinfo.

38. PBwiki. *About PBwiki*. Retrieved May 8, 2008, from http://pbwiki .com/content/team.

39. Educause Learning Initiative. (2005, July). *7 things you should know about . . . Wikis*. Retrieved January 27, 2010, from http://net.educause.edu/ ir/library/pdf/ELI7004.pdf

40. iLife Support. *GarageBand Support Working With Podcasts*. Retrieved June 18, 2009, from http://www.apple.com/support/garageband/ podcasts/

41. Webster, T. (2008). *The Podcast Consumer Revealed 2008*. Retrieved December 17, 2009, from Edison Research: http://www.edisonresearch.com/ home/archives/2008/04/the_podcast_con_1.ph p

42. Farivar, C. (2005, April 22). *Start your own Podcast*. Macworld. Retrieved June 18, 2009, from http://www.macworld.com/article/44428/ 2005/04/iunecreate.html

43. iTunes. *FAQ's: For Podcast Fans*. Retrieved June 18, 2009, from http://www.apple.com/itunes/whatson/podcasts/fanfaq.html

44. Holtz, S. (2007). *How to Do Everything with Podcasting*. p. 4. New York: McGraw Hill.

45. Cornell Enterprise: Fall 2008. *Inside Johnson: Faculty podcast series*. Retrieved June 18, 2009, from http://www.johnson.cornell.edu/alumni/ enterprise/fall2008/departments2_facul typodcast.html

46. Apple. *In 12 Minutes and 31 Seconds, You Can Start Podcasting*. Retrieved June 18, 2009, from http://www.seminars.apple.com/seminars online/podcastproducer/apple/

47. iLife. *GarageBand '09*. Retrieved January 27, 2010, from http:// www.apple.com/ilife/garageband

48. Cisco. Flip Video. *Introducting the all new Mino HD now playing: you.our sleekest widescreen yet* Retrieved March 17, 2010, from Flip Video: http://www.theflip.com/en-us/

49. iLife Support. *GarageBand Support: Recording Your Podcast*. Retrieved June 18, 2009, from http://www.apple.com/support/garageband/ podcasts/recording/

· 50. Google FeedBurner Help. *Feed 101*. Retrieved January 27, 2010, from http://www.google.com/support/feedburner/bin/answer.py?hl = en&answer = 79408

51. University of Wisconsin–Madison. *Earthwatch Radio Podcasts*. Retrieved December 12, 2009, from http://www.podcastdirectory.com/pod casts/2480

52. podCast411. *The 411 on podCasts, podCasters & podCasting*. Retrieved December 12, 2009 from http://www.podcast411.com/page2.html

53. iTunes. *Making a Podcast*. Retrieved July 17, 2009, from http:// www.apple.com/itunes/whatson/podcasts/specs.html

54. Google FeedBurner Help. *PingShot Overview and FAQ*. Retrieved January, 27, 2010, from http://www.google.com/support/feedburner/bin/ answer.py?hl = en&answer = 78988

55. McGirt, E. (2008, March 19). The Brand Called Obama. Retrieved August 8, 2009, from *Fast Company*: http://www.fastcompany.com/node/ 754505

56. YouTube Report 2009. (2009, July 2). *YouTube Now and in the Future—YouTube For Business*. Retrieved July 25, 2009, from http://youtube report2009.com/youtube-now-and-in-the-future-youtube-for-business/

57. Nielsenwire. (2009, June 15). *Time Spent Viewing Video Online Up 49 Percent*. Retrieved July 25, 2009, from http://blog.nielsen.com/nielsen-wire/online_mobile/time-spent-viewing-video-online-up-49-percent/

58. Heffernan, V. (2009, April 12). *The YouTube Presidency*. New York Times Magazine, p. 15–17.

59. YouTube. *BarackObama.com*. Retrieved July 25, 2009, from http:// www.youtube.com/user/BarackObamadotcom?PHPSESSI . . .

60. Berlin, L. (2008, October 26). If No One Sees It, Is It an Invention? Retrieved January 27, 2010, from the *New York Times*: http://www.nytimes .com/2008/10/26/business/26proto.html

61. Lee, J. (2007, December 21). *Head Tracking for Desktop VR Displays Using the WiiRemote*. Retrieved January 27, 2009, from http://www.you tube.com/watch?v = Jd3-eiid-Uw

62. Berlin. If No One Sees It, Is It an Invention?

63. Hardesty, L. *TR35: 2008 Young Innovator*. Retrieved December 13, 2009, from Technology Review: http://www.technologyreview.com/TR35/ Profile.aspx?TRID = 726

64. Berlin. If No One Sees It, Is It an Invention?

65. Penn State Education Technology Services. (2008, June 2). *PSU Teaching and Learning on YouTube*. Retrieved July 25, 2009, from http:// ets.tlt.psu.edu/announcements/psu-teaching-and-learning-on-youtube/

66. Pausch, R. (2007, September 18). *Randy Pausch Last Lecture: Achieving Your Childhood Dreams*. Retrieved December 13, 2009, from http://www.youtube.com/watch?v = ji5_MqicxSo

67. SciVee. *Making Science Visible*. Retrieved January 27, 2010, from http://www.scivee.tv/about_bk

68. Read, B. (2007, August, 21). Scientists Get a YouTube of Their Own. Retrieved January 27, 2010, from the *Chronicle of Higher Education*: http://chronicle.com/blogPost/Scientists-Get-a-YouTube-of/3277/

69. Stone, B. (2009, March 29). Is Facebook Growing Up Too Fast? Retrieved January 27, 2010, from the *New York Times*: http://www.nytimes.com/2009/03/29/technology/internet/29face.html?_r = 1&pagewanted = print

70. McLeary, P. (2007, April 18). What Happens When an i-Reporter Gets Hurt? Retrieved January 27, 2010, from the *Columbia Journalism Review*: http://www.cjr.org/behind_the_news/what_happens_when_an_ireporter.php

Conclusion

Share your good work. Academics, scholars, and researchers have a passion for learning and discovery. So does the public. You can advance dialogue, understanding, and meaningful change by sharing what you know with those outside your discipline, classroom, lab, or institution. This can contribute to individuals, communities, businesses, and governments making better choices that are based on facts. It also can add to your institution's or organization's name recognition and reputation.

Effectively communicating information is an art and a science. Working with media is often key to building a dynamic and successful communications program. Good media coverage is earned. To secure it, you first need a story that is news and relates to the interest of the audience you are trying to reach. In other words, you need to answer "Why should these listeners or readers care?" Once you've defined your story, it then needs to be told in a concise and interesting way. Avoid jargon. Bring the reader into the story through thoughtful use of metaphors and sound bites. These guideposts focus the attention of the reader or listener and convey essential information in telling your story.

Don't let ego hold you back or get ahead of you. Tell your story with truth and passion, and make smart use of the communication resources available to you. Share your knowledge. Be a voice in changing the world. As Emerson said, you are "the world's eye" and "the world's heart."

APPENDIX A

Selected Major Television and Radio Programs That Use Guest Interviews

Television:
ABC
Good Morning America
News, current events, entertainment
Weekdays, 7 a.m. to 9 a.m.
77 West 66th Street, New York, NY 10023
212-456-5900
http://abcnews.go.com/GMA/

Nightline
News, current events
Weekdays, 11:35 p.m. to 12:05 a.m.
1717 DeSales Street, NW, Washington, DC 20036
202-222-7000
http://abcnews.go.com/Nightline/

CBS
The Early Show
News, current events, entertainment
Weekdays, 7 a.m. to 9 a.m.
524 West 57th Street, New York, NY 10019
212-975-2824
http://www.cbsnews.com/sections/earlyshow/main500202.shtml

CNN
American Morning
News, current events, entertainment

Weekdays, 6 a.m. to 9 a.m.
One Time Warner Center, New York, NY 10019
212/275-7820
http://amfix.blogs.cnn.com/

Fox
Fox and Friends
News, current events, entertainment
Weekdays, 6 a.m. to 9a.m.
News Corporation, 1211 Avenue of the Americas, New York, NY 10036
212-301-3000
http://www.foxnews.com/foxfriends/

MSNBC
Morning Joe
News, current events, entertainment
Weekdays, 6 a.m. to 9 a.m.
30 Rockefeller Plaza, New York, NY 10112
212-664-4444
http://www.msnbc.msn.com/id/3036789/

NBC
Today
News, current events, entertainment
Weekdays, 7 a.m. to 11 a.m.
General Electric Company, 30 Rockefeller Plaza, New York, NY 10112
212-664-4602
http://today.msnbc.msn.com/

PBS
PBS NewsHour
News, current events, politics
Weekdays, 6 p.m. to 7 p.m.
3620 27th Street, Arlington, VA 22206
703-998-2150
http://www.pbs.org/newshour/

Charlie Rose
News, current events, culture, politics
Weekdays, check local listing
731 Lexington Avenue, New York, NY 10022
212-617-1600
http://www.charlierose.com/

Radio:
National Public Radio
All Things Considered
News, current events, culture, politics
Weekdays, 4 p.m. to 6 p.m.
NPR, 635 Massachusetts Avenue, NW, Washington, DC 20001
202-513-2110
http://www.npr.org/allthingsconsidered

Morning Edition
News, current events, culture, politics
Weekdays, 5 a.m. to 7 a.m.
NPR, 635 Massachusetts Avenue, NW, Washington, DC 20001
202-513-2150
http://www.npr.org/morningedition

The Talk of the Nation
News, current events, culture, politics
Weekdays, 2 p.m. to 4 p.m.
NPR, 635 Massachusetts Avenue, NW, Washington, DC 20001
202-513-2343
http://www.npr.org/totn

Fresh Air
Current events, culture
Weekdays, check local listing
WHYY, 150 North Sixth Street, Philadelphia, PA 19106
215-351-1200
http://www.npr.org/freshair

The Diane Rehm Show
News, current events, culture
Weekdays, 10 a.m. to 12 p.m.
WAMU, American University, 4000 Brandywine Street, NW,
    Washington, DC 20016
202-885-1231
http://wamu.org/programs/dr/

Science Friday
Science
Friday, 2 p.m. to 4 p.m.
4 West 43rd Street, Suite 306, New York, NY 10036
202-513-2000
http://www.sciencefriday.com/

American Public Media
Marketplace
Business, economics
Weekdays, check local listing
261 South Figueroa Street, Suite 200, Los Angeles, CA 90012
213-621-3500
http://marketplace.publicradio.org/

Public Radio International
Here & Now
News, current events, culture
Weekdays, check local listing
WBUR, 890 Commonwealth Avenue, Boston, MA 02215
617-353-0909
http://www.hereandnow.org/

Living on Earth
Environment
Weekly, check local listing
20 Holland Street, Suite 408, Somerville, MA 02144
617-776-2730
http://www.livingonearth.org/

Voice of America
Our World
Science and technology
Saturday, 3 a.m., 5 a.m., 3:30 p.m. Sunday, 4 a.m., 9 a.m., 11 a.m.
Voice of America, 330 Independence Avenue, SW, Washington, DC
    20037
202-203-4000
http://www.voanews.com/english/science/ourworld.cfm

APPENDIX B

Canadian Media

Selected Canadian Television Programs with Guest Interviews

CBC

The Fifth Estate
News, current events
Friday 9 p.m. to 10 p.m.
250 Front Street
P.O. Box 500, Station "C"
Toronto, ON M5W 1E4
416-205-6663
http://www.cbc.ca/fifth/
blog: http://www.cbc.ca/fifth/discussion/

The Hour
News, current events, entertainment
Weeknights 11 p.m. to 12 a.m.
c/o CBC Television
P.O. Box 500, Station "A"
Toronto, ON M5W 1E6
Email: thehour@cbc.ca
http://www.cbc.ca/thehour/index.html

Mansbridge One on One
News, current events, entertainment
Sunday, 3:30 a.m. to 4:00 a.m., Monday, 4:00 a.m. to 4:30 a.m.
250 Front Street
P.O. Box 500, Station "C"

Toronto, ON M5W 1E4
416-205-3311
http://www.cbc.ca/mansbridge/

Power and Politics with Evan Solomon
News
Weeknights 5 p.m. to 7 p.m. (CBC News Network)
Contact: http://www.cbc.ca/contact/
http://www.cbc.ca/programguide/program/power_
   politics_with_evan_solomon

CTV

Canada AM
News, current events, entertainment
MondayFriday 6 a.m. to 9 a.m.
Assignment Desk
Canada AM, CTV
P.O. Box 9, Station o
Toronto, ON M4A 2M9
Story ideas: am@ctv.ca
http://www.ctv.ca/canadaam/

W5
News, current events
Saturday 7 p.m. to 8 p.m.
W5, CTV
P.O. Box 9, Station "O"
Toronto, ON M4A 2M9
Email: W5@ctv.ca
Fax: 416-384 -5938.
http://www.ctv.ca/w5/

TVO

The Agenda with Steve Paikin
News, current affairs
Weekdays 8 p.m. to 8:30 p.m., repeated 11 p.m. to 11:30 p.m.
PO Box 200, Station Q
Toronto, ON M4T 2T1
2180 Yonge Street
Toronto, Ontario M4S 2B9
(416) 484-2600
http://www.tvo.org/cfmx/tvoorg/theagenda/

Selected Canadian Radio Programs with Guest Interviews

CBC

As it Happens
News, current events, entertainment
Weeknights 6:30 p.m. to 8:00 p.m.
Box 500 Station A
Toronto, Ontario M5W 1E6
Courier address:
205 Wellington Street West
Toronto, ON M5V 3G7
Fax: (416) 205-2639
Phone-Talkback (Toll free):
1-866-481-5718
http://www.cbc.ca/asithappens/index.html

The Current
News, current events
Weekdays 8:30 a.m. to 10:00 a.m.
P.O. Box 500, Station A
Toronto, ON M5W 1E6
Feedback line: 1-877-287-7366
Fax: 416-205-6461
Twitter: @TheCurrentCBC
http://www.cbc.ca/thecurrent/

Quirks and Quarks
Science, technology, medicine & the environment
Saturday 12:06 p.m. to 1:00 p.m.
250 Front Street
P.O. Box 500 Station A
Toronto, ON M5W 1E6
Phone: 416-205-6124
Fax: 416-205-2372
http://www.cbc.ca/quirks/index.html

Q with Jian Ghomeshi
Arts, Culture, Entertainment
Weekdays 10 a.m. and 10 p.m.
P.O.Box 500
Station A

Toronto, ON M5W 1E6
Phone: 416-205-3700
Fax: 416-205-6040
Blog: http://www.cbc.ca/q/blog/
http://www.cbc.ca/q/

Here and Now
News, current events
Weekdays 3 p.m. to 6 p.m.
P.O. Box 500, Station "A"
Toronto, ON 5W 1E6
By Courier:
205 Wellington St. W.
Room 3H100D
Toronto, ON M5V 3G7
Comments: 416-205-2700
http://www.cbc.ca/hereandnowtoronto/

The Sunday Edition
Culture and current events
P.O. Box 500, Station "A"
Toronto, ON M5W 1E6
Sundays 9 a.m. to 12 p.m.
416-205-3700 (Audience Inquiries)
email: fill out form on website
http://www.cbc.ca/thesundayedition/

Spark
Technology and culture
Tuesdays 3 p.m. to 4 p.m.
Email spark@cbc.ca
Twitter: @SparkCBC
Phone: 1-877-34-SPARK
http://www.cbc.ca/spark/

Fresh Air
News, current affairs, culture, entertainment
Saturday and Sunday 6 a.m. to 9 a.m.
P.O. Box 500, Station "A"
Toronto, ON M5W 1E6
Courier Address:
205 Wellington St. W.
Room 3H200K

Toronto, ON M5V 3G7
416-205-3700
Email: form on contact page
http://www.cbc.ca/freshair/

Cross Country Checkup
Current Affairs
Sunday 4 p.m. to 6 p.m.
P.O. Box 500, Station "A"
Toronto, ON M5W 1E6
Toll-free number (during the broadcast only):
1-888-416-8333
Email: checkup@cbc.ca
http://www.cbc.ca/checkup/

Tapestry
Spirituality and Religion
Sunday, 2:05 p.m. to 3 p.m., Thursday 3:05 p.m. to 4 p.m.
P.O. Box 500, Station "A"
Toronto, ON M5W 1E6
416 205-3700
email: form on contact page
http://www.cbc.ca/tapestry/index.html

CBC Main Addresses in Canada

Ottawa Production Centre (Head Office)
181 Queen Street
P.O. Box 3220, Station "C"
Ottawa, ON K1Y 1E4
Phone: 613-288-6000 (general inquiries)
Phone: 613-288-6455 (TDD)
E-mail: liaison@cbc.ca

Canadian Broadcasting Centre, Toronto
250 Front Street West
P.O. Box 500, Station "A"
Toronto, ON M5W 1E6
Phone: 416-205-3311 (general inquiries)
Phone: 416-205-6688 (TDD)

Toll Free: 1-866-306-4636
E-mail: cbcinput@cbc.ca

Maison de Radio-Canada, Montréal
1400 René-Lévesque Boulevard East
P.O. Box 6000
Montréal, QC H3C 3A8
Phone: 514- 597-6000 (general inquiries)
Phone: 514- 597-6013 (TDD)
Toll Free: 1-866-306-4636
E-mail: auditoire@radio-canada.ca

Regional Offices

Newfoundland and Labrador
95 University Avenue
P.O. Box 12010, Station "A"
St. John's, NL A1B 1Z4
Phone: 709-576-5000 (general inquiries)

Nova Scotia
Halifax
Radio Building: 5600 Sackville Street
Television Building: 1840 Bell Road
P.O. Box 3000
Halifax, NS B3J 3E9
Phone: 902- 420-8311 (general inquiries)
Sydney
285 Alexandra Street
Sydney, NS B1S 2E8
Phone: 902-539-5050 (general inquiries)

Prince Edward Island
P.O. Box 2230
Charlottetown, PEI C1A 8B9
Phone: (902) 629-6400 (general enquiries)

New Brunswick
Moncton
250 Université Avenue
P.O. Box 950
Moncton, NB E1C 8N8
Phone: 506-853-6666 (general inquiries)

Fredericton
1160 Regent Street
P.O. Box 2200, MPO
Fredericton, NB E3B 5G4
Phone: 506-451-4000 (general inquiries)
Saint John
560 Principal Street, Suite 200
P.O. Box 2358
Saint John, NB E2L 3V6
Phone: 506-632 7710 (general inquiries)

Québec
Québec City
888 St-Jean Street
P.O. Box 18,800
Québec City, QC G1K 9L4
Phone: 418-654-1341 (general inquiries)

Ontario
Windsor
825 Riverside Drive West
Windsor, ON N9A 5K9
Phone: 519-255-3411 (general inquiries)
Sudbury
15 Mackenzie Street
Sudbury, ON P3C 4Y1
Phone: 705-688-3200 (general inquiries)

Manitoba
541 Portage Avenue
P.O. Box 160
Winnipeg, MB R3C 2H1
Phone: 204-788-3222 (general inquiries)

Saskatchewan
Regina
2440 Broad Street
P.O. Box 540
Regina, SK S4P 4A1
Phone: 306-347-9540 (general inquiries)
Saskatoon
144-2nd Avenue South
Saskatoon, SK S7K 1K5
Phone: 306-956-7400 (general inquiries)

Alberta
Edmonton
10062—102nd Avenue
123, Edmonton City Centre
P.O. Box 555
Edmonton, AB T5J 2P4
Phone: 780-468-7500 (general inquiries)
Calgary
1724 Westmount Blvd. N.W.
P.O. Box 2640
Calgary, AB T2P 2M7
Phone: 403-521-6000 (general inquiries)

British Columbia
775 Cambie Street
P.O. Box 4600
Vancouver, BC V6B 4AZ
Phone: 604-662-6000 (general inquiries)

CBC North
Yellowknife
5002 Forrest Drive
P.O. Box 160
Yellowknife, NT X1A 2N2
Phone: 867-920-5400 (general inquiries)
Whitehorse
3103 – 3rd Avenue
Whitehorse, YK Y1A 2A2
Phone: 867-668-8400 (general inquiries)

Selected Canadian Journals and Newspapers

Media Source

Sources
Media Source
489 College Street
Suite 305
Toronto, ON M6G 1A5
416- 964-7799
Fax: 416-964-8763

Email: sources@sources.ca
http://sources.ca/

Newspapers

Globe and Mail
National Newspaper
444 Front Street West,
Toronto, ON M5V 2S9
The main telephone number is 1-416-585-5000
http://v1.theglobeandmail.com/help/contact-paper/
http://v1.theglobeandmail.com/help/contact-web/
Special Magazines:
Report on Business
Canadian University Report Magazine
http://www.theglobeandmail.com/

National Post
National newspaper
1450 Don Mills Road, Suite 300
Don Mills, ON M3B 3R5
Phone: 416-383-2300 (general inquiries)
Fax: 416-383-2305
News tips only: 416-386-2600
Contacts on internet: http://www.nationalpost.com/contact/index.html
http://www.nationalpost.com/

Financial Post
Business News
Published by Globe and Mail
Phone: 416-383-2300
Fax: 416-383-2305
http://www.financialpost.com/

Toronto Star
Newspaper – Ontario
General inquiries:
Toronto Star
One Yonge Street
Toronto, ON M5E 1E6
416-367-2000
Newsroom:
Phone: 416-869-4300

Fax: 416-869-4328
email city@thestar.ca
Contact page: http://www.thestar.com/contactus
http://www.thestar.com/

Le Devoir
French-language newspaper
2050, Bleury, 9th Floor
Montreal (Quebec) H3A 3M9
514 985-3333
http://www.ledevoir.com/

Montreal Gazette
Global TV Montreal
1010 Ste-Catherine St. West
Suite 200
Montreal, QC H3B 5L1
Phone: 514-521-4323
Fax: 514-590 4060
http://www.montrealgazette.com/

Vancouver Sun
The Vancouver Sun
#1—200 Granville Street
Vancouver BC V6C 3N3
http://www.vancouversun.com/index.html

Magazines

Macleans
News, current affairs, entertainment
One Mount Pleasant Road
11th floor
Toronto, ON M4Y 2Y5
Phone: 1-800-268-9119
or 416-764-1300
Fax: 416-764-1332
http://www2.macleans.ca/contactus/
http://www2.macleans.ca/

Walrus
Politics, culture, environment
Submission guidelines: http://www.walrusmagazine.com/queries/

The Walrus
19 Duncan Street, Suite 101
Toronto, ON, M5H 3H1
Fax 416-971-8768.
Blog: http://www.walrusmagazine.com/blogs/
http://www.walrusmagazine.com/

Journals

Academic Matters
Journal of Higher Education
http://www.academicmatters.ca/
published by:
OCUFA
83 Yonge Street, Suite 300
Toronto, ON M5C 1S8
Phone: 416-979-2117
Fax: 416-593-5607
Web site: www.ocufa.on.ca

Literary Review of Canada
Social, political, cultural commentary
581 Markham Street, Suite 3A
Toronto, ON M6G 2L7
review@lrcreview.com
Phone: 416-531-1483
Fax: 416-531-1612
Contact page: http://reviewcanada.ca/contact/

ITBusiness.ca
IT World Canada Inc.
55 Town Centre Court, Suite 302
Scarborough, ON M1P 4X4
416-290-0240
email: info@itbusiness.ca
http://www.itbusiness.ca/it/client/en/ComputerCanada/Home.asp

Canadian Foreign Policy
Dunton Tower, Room 2116
Carleton University
1125 Colonel By Drive
Ottawa, ON K1S5B6
Phone: 613-520-6696

Fax: 613-520-3981
E-mail: cfp@carleton.ca
http://www.carleton.ca/cfpj/

Anthropoligica
Canadian Anthropology Society
Andrew Lyons
Department of Anthropology
Wilfred Laurier Universit
2-139 DAWB
75 University Avenue West
Waterloo, ON N2L 3C5
Phone: 519-886-7975
http://anthropologica.ca/index.htm

CMAJ
Canadian Medical Association Journal
Canadian Medical Association Journal Staff
1867 Alta Vista Drive
Ottawa ON K1G 5W8
Phone: 866-971-9171 x2295
Fax 613 565-5471
http://www.cmaj.ca

Alternatives
Environmental Studies Journal
Faculty of Environmental Studies
University of Waterloo
Waterloo, Ontario N2L 3G1
Phone: 519-888-4442
Toll free: 866-437-2587
Fax: 519-746-0292
http://www.alternativesjournal.ca/

Canadian Historical Review
Candis Green
Editorial Assistant/Assistante à la rédaction
University of Toronto Press Journals Division
5201 Dufferin St.
Toronto ON M3H 5T8
cgreen@utpress.utoronto.ca
416-667-7777 x 7994

Fax: 416-667-7881
See submission guidelines:
http://presto.utpjournals.com/index.php/CHR/information/authors

Canadian Journal of Political Science
Csaba Nikolenyi
Concordia University
Montreal, Quebec
csaba@alcor.concordia.ca
submissions, see: http://www.editorialmanager.com/cjps-rcsp/
http://www.cpsa-acsp.ca/cjps.shtml

Canadian Journal of Sociology
The Editor
Canadian Journal of Sociology
Department of Sociology
University of Alberta
Edmonton, AB T6G 2H4
email: cjscopy@gpu.srv.ualberta.ca
http://ejournals.library.ualberta.ca/index.php/CJS/index

Biochemistry and Cell Biology
University of Manitoba
Room T253-770 Bannatyne Ave.
Winnipeg, MB, R3E 0W3
204-977-5695
204-977-5697
bcbeo@cc.umanitoba.ca

Botany, formerly Canadian Journal of Botany
University of Guelph
Molecular and Cellular Biology Science Complex
581 Gordon Street
Guelph, ON N1G 2W1
519-824-4120 x 54597
519-827-9549
canjbot@uoguelph.ca

Canadian Journal of Chemistry
University of Western Ontario
Department of Chemistry
1151 Richmond Street
London, ON N6A 5B7

519-661-2111 x 86359
519-434-9214
canjchem@bell.net

Canadian Journal of Civil Engineering
University of British Columbia
Department of Civil Engineering
Vancouver, British Columbia, Canada
V6T 1Z4
604-822-2523
604-822-0568
cjce@civil.ubc.ca

Canadian Journal of Earth Sciences
Canadian Journal of Earth Sciences
Editorial office
9323—96 street
Edmonton, AB, T6C 3Y6
780-468-3271
1-780-468-3918
cjes.editor@ubc.ca

Canadian Journal of Physics
St. Francis Xavier University
ATTN Nicole Huskins
Rm 3055 Physical Science Complex
PO Box 5000
Antigonish, Nova Scotia, B2G 2W5
902-867-5302
902-867-2439
canjphys@stfx.ca

University Affairs
350 Albert Street, suite 600
Ottawa, Ontario K1R 1B1
Phone: 613-563-1236
Fax: 613-563-9745
ua@aucc.ca
http://www.universityaffairs.ca/letters-and-submissions.aspx
www.universityaffairs.ca

APPENDIX C

British Media

Selected British Newspapers

The Daily Mail
Associated Newspapers Limited
Northcliffe House
2 Derry Street
London W8 5TT
http://www.dailymail.co.uk/home/article-1227210/Contact-Us.html
Phone: 020 7938 6000
Email: news@dailymail.co.uk
Blogs: http://www.dailymail.co.uk/debate/blogs/index.html

The Daily Telegraph
111 Buckingham Palace Road
London SW1W 0DT
http://www.telegraph.co.uk/topics/about-us/3489870/Contact-us.html?/
Phone: 020 7931 2000
Email: dtnews@telegraph.co.uk
Blogs: http://blogs.telegraph.co.uk/

The Economist
25 St James's Street
London SW1A 1HG
http://www.economist.com/help/DisplayHelp.cfm?folder = 663392
Phone: 020 7839 2968
Email: letters@economist.com
Blogs: www.economist.com/blogs/

The Guardian
Kings Place
90 York Way
London N1 9GU
http://www.guardian.co.uk/gu_contacts/0,,180767,00.html
Phone: 020 3353 2000
Email: editor@guardianunlimited.co.uk
Blogs: http://www.guardian.co.uk/tone/blog
Also have an Educational Supplement

The Independent
2 Derry Street
London W8 5HF
http://www.independent.co.uk/service/contact-us-759589.html
Phone: 020 7005 2000
Email: j.leach@independent.co.uk
Blogs: http://blogs.independent.co.uk/independent/2008/11/keen-on-
new-m-3.html

The Independent on Sunday
2 Derry Street
London W8 5HF
http://www.independent.co.uk/service/contact-us-759589.html
Phone: 020 7005 2000
Email: j.leach@independent.co.uk
Blogs: http://blogs.independent.co.uk/independent/2008/11/keen-on-
new-m-3.html

The Mail on Sunday
Associated Newspapers Limited
Northcliffe House
2 Derry Street
London W8 5TT
http://www.dailymail.co.uk/home/article-1227210/Contact-Us.h tml
Phone: 020 7938 6899
Email: news@mailonsunday.co.uk
Blogs: http://www.mailonsunday.co.uk/debate/blogs/index.html

The Observer
Kings Place
90 York Way
London N1 9GU
http://observer.guardian.co.uk/contacts/

Phone: 020 7278 2332
Email: reader@observer.co.uk
Blogs – yes http://www.guardian.co.uk/news/observerblog

The Sunday Telegraph
111 Buckingham Palace Road
London SW1W 0DT
http://www.telegraph.co.uk/topics/about-us/3489870/Contact-us.html?/
Phone: 020 7931 2000
Email: dtnews@telegraph.co.uk
Blogs: http://blogs.telegraph.co.uk/

The Sunday Times
1 Pennington Street
London E1 9XN
http://www.timesonline.co.uk/tol/tools_and_services/services/
    contact_us/
Phone: 020 7782 5000
Email: news desk@sunday-times.co.uk
Blogs: http://www.timesonline.co.uk/tol/comment/blogs/

The Times
1 Pennington Street
London E1 9XN
http://www.timesonline.co.uk/tol/tools_and_services/services/
    contact_us/
Phone: 020 7782 5000
Email: home.news@thetimes.co.uk
Blogs: http://www.timesonline.co.uk/tol/comment/blogs/

Times Literary Supplement
1 Pennington Street
London E1 9XN
http://entertainment.timesonline.co.uk/tol/arts_and_entertainment/
    the_tls/article2385089.ece
Phone: 020 7782 5000
Email: letters@the-tls.co.uk

Blogs: http://entertainment.timesonline.co.uk/tol/arts_and_entertain
    ment/the_tls/article5467502.ece

Times Higher Education Supplement
26 Red Lion Square

London WC1R 4HQ
http://www.timeshighereducation.co.uk/contacts.asp?navCode = 94
Phone: 020 3194 3000
Email: webmaster@timeshighereducation.co.uk
Blogs: http://www.timeshighereducation.co.uk/section.asp?
    navcode = 116

New Scientist
Lacon House
84 Theobald's Road
London WC1X 8NS
http://www.newscientist.com/contact/us
Phone: 01444 475 636
Email: editor@mediaguardian.co.uk
Blogs: http://www.newscientist.com/section/blogs

Nature
The Macmillan Building
4 Crinan Street
London N1 9XW
http://www.nature.com/npg_/contact/index.html
Phone: 020 7833 4000
Email: informationandservices@npg.com
Blogs: http://blogs.nature.com/

The Sun
1 Virginia Street
Wapping
London E98 1SN
http://www.thesun.co.uk/sol/homepage/article296174.ece
Phone: 020 7782 4100
Email: corporate.info@the-sun.co.uk
Blogs: www.thesun.co.uk/sol/homepage/blogs

The Mirror
1 Canada Square
Canary Wharf
London E14 5AP
http://www.mirror.co.uk/about-the-mirror/contact-us/
Phone: 020 7293 3409
Email: mirrornews@mgn.co.uk
Blogs: http://blogs.mirror.co.uk

The Newspaper Society
8th Floor
St Andrew's House
18–20 St Andrew Street
London EC4A 3AY
http://www.newspapersoc.org.uk/Default.aspx?page=1459
Phone: 020 7632 7401
Email: ns@newspapersoc.org.uk

Chemistry World
Royal Society of Chemistry
Burlington House
London W1J 0BA
http://www.rsc.org/AboutUs/contacts/
Phone: 020 7437 8883
Email: chemistry world email via website entry
Blogs: http://prospect.rsc.org/blogs/cw/

Construction News
Greater London House
Hampstead Road
London NW1 7EJ
http://info.cnplus.co.uk/company/contactus
Email: cn@subscription.co.uk
Blogs: http://www.cnplus.co.uk/home/blogs/

Selected British Radio Programs with Guest Interviews

BBC RADIO 1
The Chris Moyles Show
News, entertainment, current affairs
Weekdays 6:30 a.m. to 10:00 a.m.
BBC Radio 1
Yalding House
152–156 Great Portland Street
London
W1N 4DJ
http://www.bbc.co.uk/programmes/b00pwrbt
Email: chris.moyles@bbc.co.uk
Text: 81199 during show hours Mon–Fri
Blog: http://www.bbc.co.uk/radio1/blogs/

BBC RADIO 2
The Chris Evans Breakfast Show
News, current affairs, entertainment
Weekdays 7:00 am–9:30 am
BBC Radio 2
BBC broadcasting House
Portland Place
London W1A 1AA
http://www.bbc.co.uk/radio2/
Email: chris.evans@bbc.co.uk
Text during show times: 88291
Blog: http://www.bbc.co.uk/blogs/chrisevans/

BBC RADIO 3
Breakfast
News, current affairs, politics, entertainment
Weekdays 7 a.m. to 10 a.m.
BBC Radio 3Breakfast
Room 1015
BBC broadcasting House
Portland Place
London W1A 1AA
http://www.bbc.co.uk/radio3
Email: 3breakfast@bbc.co.uk
Phone: 03700 100 300
Blog: http://www.bbc.co.uk/blogs/radio3/

BBC RADIO 4
The World at One
News both national and international
Weekdays 1:00 p.m. to 1:30 p.m.
BBC Radio 4
The World at One
BBC Broadcasting House
Portland Place
London W1A 1AA
http://www.bbc.co.uk/radio4/
Podcast: http://www.bbc.co.uk/radio4/podcasts/

BBC RADIO 4
Women's Hour
Cultural debate and entertainment

Weekdays 10 a.m. to 10:45 a.m.
BBC Radio 4
Women's Hour
BBC Broadcasting House
Portland Place
London W1A 1AA
http://www.bbc.co.uk/radio4/
Podcast: http://www.bbc.co.uk/radio4/podcasts/

CAPITAL FM RADIO
Breakfast Show
News, current affairs, entertainment
Weekdays 7 a.m. to 9 a.m.
95.8 Capital FM
30 Leicester Square
London WC2H 7LA
http://www.capitalfm.com/
Phone: 020 7766 6000
Fax: 020 7766 6100
Text: 83958
Email: info@capitalfm.com

BBC RADIO 5LIVE
5 Live Breakfast
Weekday mornings 6 a.m. to 9 a.m.
News, current events and sport
BBC Radio5 Live
Television Centre
Wood Lane
London W12 7RJ
Email: livesey@bbc.co.uk
Phone: 0500 909 693
http://www.bbc.co.uk/5live/
Podcast: http://www.bbc.co.uk/5live/podcasts/

BBC RADIO 1XTRA
Breakfast Show With Trevor Nelson
Weekday mornings 7 a.m. to 10 a.m.
Entertainment, news, current affairs
1Xtra
PO Box 1X
London W1A

Studio text: 88111
Switch board: 020 8743 8000
Email: 1xtra@bbc.co.uk
http://www.bbc.co.uk/1xtra/

Selected British Television Programs with Guest Interviews

BBC ONE
The One Show
News, current events, entertainment
Weeknights 7 p.m. to 7:30 p.m.
BBC One
Television Centre
Wood Lane
London W12 7RJ
http://www.bbc.co.uk/bbcone
Blog: http://www.bbc.co.uk/blogs/theoneshow/backstage-and-celebs/

BBC ONE
Breakfast
Weekdays 6 a.m. to 9:15 a.m.
BBC One
Television Centre
Wood Lane
London W12 7RJ
Phone: 03700 100 124
Email: bbcbreakfast@bbc.co.uk
http://news.bbc.co.uk/1/hi/programmes/breakfast/default.stm
Blog: http://news.bbc.co.uk/1/hi/talking_point/default.stm

BBC ONE
Watchdog
Topical reports and investigations
Wednesdays 8 p.m. to 9 p.m.
BBC One
Television Centre
Wood Lane
London W12 7RJ
http://www.bbc.co.uk/watchdog
Blog: http://www.bbc.co.uk/blogs/watchdog/

BBC TWO
Newsnight
News, current affairs, politics
Weeknights 10.30 p.m. to 11:20 p.m.
BBC Newsnight
Room G680
Television Centre
Wood Lane
London W12 7RJ
http://www.bbc.co.uk/bbctwo
Email: NewsnightInvestigations@bbc.co.uk
General inquiries to: newsnight@bbc.co.uk
Blog: http://www.bbc.co.uk/blogs/newsnight/

BBC TWO
University Challenge
Academic quiz show
Mondays 8 p.m to 9 p.m.
BBC Two
Television Centre
Wood Lane
London W12 7RJ
http://www.bbc.co.uk/bbctwo

ITV ONE
Night watch with Steve Scott
Real life medical emergencies
Tuesdays 12.30 a.m. to 1:25 a.m.
IVT1
The London Television Centre
Upper Ground
London SE1 9LT
http://www.itv.com/itv1
Email: info@itv.co.uk

ITV ONE
GMTV
News, entertainment, current affairs
Weekdays 6 a.m. to 9:25 a.m.
GMTV
Viewer Correspondence Co-ordinator
The London Television Centre

Upper Ground
London SE1 9LT
http://www.itv.com/itv1
Email: info@itv.co.uk
Phone: 0870 243 4333
Blog: http://www.gm.tv/entertainment/tv/red-nose-kilimanjaro-climb/
    33542-bens-blog.html

ITV 1
Loose Women
News, current affairs, entertainment
Weekdays 12.30 p.m. to 1:30 p.m.
Loose Women
PO BOX 56317
London SE1 9TJ
http://www.itv.com/Lifestyle/LooseWomen/default.html
Phone: 020 8532 2771 2770
Email: loose.women@itv.com
Blog: http://community.loosewomen.itv.com/service/searchEverything
    .kickAction?as = 27030&mediaType = blog&sortType = recent&
    includeBlog = on&d-7095067-p = 1

INDEX